A Tuscan Penitent

The Life and Legend of St. Margaret of Cortona

BY

FATHER CUTHBERT

Of the Order of St. Francis, Capuchin

COVER ARTWORK BY
RAFAEL FERRAN

BURNS & OATES
28 ORCHARD STREET
LONDON

BENZIGER BROS.
NEW YORK, CINCINNATI
CHICAGO

1907

" Her body, having been embalmed and clothed in a purple robe, they buried it in a new sepulchre, many clerics and religious being present, and here, according to the promises made to her by God, many miracles were wrought."
See p. 291.

FRONTISPIECE

To B.

" Mary stood at the Sepulchre without, weeping . . . Jesus saith to her: 'Mary.' She turning, saith to Him : 'Rabboni.'"

Table of Principal Contents.

Contents.

Contents.

Contents.

Saint Margaret of Cortona :
Her Life.

MARGARET OF CORTONA was born in the year
1247 at Laviano, a little town in Tuscany.
Her father was a small farmer, whose chief
thought was for his farm and the soil he
tilled. Of her mother we know only that
she died when her daughter was but seven
years old, and that she was a good woman of
simple faith. "O Lord Jesus, I beseech
Thee for the salvation of all whom Thou
wouldst have me pray for," was a prayer she
impressed upon the memory of her daughter,
a prayer which Margaret never forgot. And
without doubt the thought of her mother was
a saving influence in Margaret's life. Two
years after her mother's death, Tancred, her
father, took to himself another wife, and with
that Margaret's history may be said to begin.

The situation is not difficult to reconstruct.
A high-spirited, sensitive girl, full of vitality,

her whole being athirst for life ; and a stepmother whose nature had no response for the
girl's, a woman who would brook no contra-
diction, who worshipped the respectabilities
and the order of her own household, and expected others to walk in the narrow way of
her own decalogue. With two such natures
brought into daily contact, you may forecast
disaster. Nor could the father's influence
have availed much, even had he had the will,
to smooth his child's path. He had committed the error of marrying a woman who
must misunderstand his child. Consciously
or unconsciously, he had by that act sacrificed his daughter to his own pleasure or
convenience ; perhaps he had not thought of
her at all in his anxiety to provide his household with a careful mistress. At any rate,
such evidence as we have points to the con-
clusion that the new wife ruled her husband
as well as his farm-house, and that Margaret
was left to bear her burden as best she might.

Had Margaret's home-life been different,
had she, as she grew from a child into a
woman, known a mother's understanding, love
and patience, it is probable that Cortona
would have lacked its most illustrious Saint.
" Happy is the nation that has no history " ;
yes, but that depends upon the point of view.

Would it have been better for Margaret had a mother's love shielded her? She would have been saved the bitter tears of repentance; but would she in the end have been as true and noble a woman? Would her life have profited the world as it actually has? The question is not idle if it teaches us to see, even amid the worst miseries of earth, a providence which rebukes our own small judgments. There are characters—who has not known them?—that can only be wrought into high nobility and sanctity by humiliation and repentance. There are many who could only attain the highest of which they are capable, by the way of repentance and the sin that needs repentance. Why it should be so is one of the mysteries of life. It may be that with these souls the shock of a great sin is needful to bring them to that humility and self-knowledge which, the Saints tell us, are the only secure foundation of virtue. However this may be, it is for us to judge the sinner tenderly and with a certain reverence; for who knows but his sin may be the way to a nobler virtue?

Margaret's surroundings, then, were such as to force to the surface the weaknesses of her character. As is clear from her own confessions, she was by nature one of those women who thirst for affection ; in whom to be loved is the imperative need of their lives. Some there are in whom this need is dominated by their primal need to love, who must pour themselves out upon others unless their faculties are to be atrophied. Such women are in a supreme sense the mothers of humanity. Not that the affection of others is to them an indifferent thing ; but that their primary need is to give rather than to receive. But there are others who lack a certain vital warmth which they seek outside themselves and for which their souls clamour with passionate appeal. For them to be loved is as the breath of life. In an atmosphere of affection they will often blossom forth into sweetness and heroic deeds. In the love which others give them they may be said to find themselves ; but until they have found what they need, their souls are athirst. Margaret was of this kind. She needed to be loved that her soul might be free ; and in her home she found not what she needed. Had she been of the weaker sort, either morally or physically, she would have accepted her lot, vegetated in spiritual barrenness, married eventually a husband of her father's choice, and lived an uneventful life with a measure of peace.

But she was not in any sense of the weaker sort : she was full of vitality and of the wish to live.   And so, not willing to be utterly repressed, she sought her life outside her home.   As yet her spiritual nature was dormant, else she might even now have found in religion the liberty of soul she found afterwards ; and in the pure love of Christ she would have been shielded against the temptations of the world.   But the hour had not yet come wherein she was to find in the higher love security against the lower.   Yet, even so, there was in Margaret no vicious taint, such as some of the later chronicles have fixed upon her.   She was fond of gaiety doubtless ; but the chronicler who describes her as an abandoned woman either had not read the story of her life fully related by Fra Giunta with evident candour, or else he distorted facts to suit a thesis, deepening the shadows of her early life that her conversion might seem the more remarkable.*   What is clear from the whole course of Fra Giunta's narrative is that Margaret even in her fall had not altogether lost her self-respect.   She was betrayed, as the *Legend* expressly tells us, under promise of marriage, by a man whom she seems to have sincerely loved.

* Wadding, *Annales, ad annum,* 1297.

She was about seventeen years when the great temptation came to her, a woman in the first bloom of womanhood, as things go in the South. She was esteemed very beautiful even in the Tuscan country where many were beautiful ; and her beauty of feature was matched by the vivacity of her wit. The tempter came in the form of a gay cavalier from the neighbourhood of Montepulciano. Some say he was the son of Guglielmo di Pecora, lord of Valiano and lands round Montepulciano, a warrior who had earned fame in the wars against the Saracens. But no hint of his identity is given by Margaret herself, or by Fra Giunta. Whoever he was, the young cavalier promised to make Margaret his wife, if she would only flee with him to his own home ; and, dazzled by the vision of a life in which love, admiration, and gaiety would be hers to the full, she consented. Under cover of night, as one biographer relates, Margaret fled from home with her lover to his house amidst the hills. The marshes of the Chiano were flooded at the time and the two lovers were nearly drowned.*

There, in his home near Montepul-

---

* This story related by Barbieri may explain the passage in *Legend* i. 2.

ciano, Margaret was installed as her lover's mistress ; and there she lived for nine years in defiance of law and convention, but with a certain meed of happiness. He gave her every pleasure she might seek, except the one thing she most earnestly wished for—the right to call herself his wife. Often during those years she begged him to marry her, and as often he pleaded delay. Meanwhile, as the *Legend* expressly says, she surrendered herself unwillingly.*

A son was born to them, and yet the promise of marriage remained unfulfilled. It was with a growing feeling of bitterness that Margaret lived on at Montepulciano. Her saving sense of shame is recorded in the story of her life as she told it to Fra Giunta in after years. But to her neighbours she gave no sign of the canker that was at the root of her gaiety; in their presence she was the pleasure-loving, imperious and witty Margaret. They might on occasion hint that she should look to her soul before it was too late, but she would not reveal to them her remorse. With a touch of sarcasm she told her mentors that they need not fear for her, for she would yet be a

* "Post obitum deceptoris tui qui novem annis *te nolente*, tuae puritati et honestati paravit insidias incessanter." (*Leg.* i. 2.)

Saint and they would come as pilgrims to
visit her shrine, with staves in their hands
and carrying pilgrims' wallets.   Yet in this
reply there was probably more than a witty
retort : it may have been at the same time a
half-shamed expression of her desire for
better things and her prevision of a penitential life as her ultimate vocation.   For she
grew accustomed to seek out quiet places
apart from the walks of man, and there
would dream of a life given up to virtue and
the praise of God.*   And she was pitiful
towards the poor and those in distress ; the
sorrow of her own soul leading her to find
with them a certain comradeship, the one
enduring thing in those days of swift dis-
illusion.

Then came the break of her life, suddenly
and without warning.   Her lover was abroad
one day when he was set upon by assassins
and done to death, perhaps as the result of a
family feud. Margaret's first intimation of
the disaster was the return of her lover's
favourite hound without its master, and the
faithful brute's distress and evident endeavour to induce her to follow him.   The
hound led the way to a neighbouring wood,
and there Margaret came upon her lover's

* *Leg.* i. 2.

mangled body. To her the murder came as a judgment from Heaven, terrible in its unexpectedness and extremity, and yet the summing-up of her own years of remorse and defiance. And the judgment had fallen not upon herself but upon her lover.

It is evidence of her inherent loyalty of soul, a loyalty which had kept her faithful to him during those nine years of broken promises, that, seeing him lying in death, she now accused herself of being the cause of his sin, and took the wrong-doing upon herself. She now felt a loathing for the beauty which had held him captive, and despised herself for the miserable triumph which had been hers in holding him fast. She returned to the house that day with her whole soul humbled to the ground, her pride broken. To herself she was a woman who had wrought death where she had sought sunshine, and not merely death, but the bitterness of hell. Nothing is told us as to the attitude his relatives took towards her, or of the sensation caused by the murder amongst her neighbours. After all, such murders were not infrequent where family and civic feuds were the order of the day. There is no sign that Margaret had earned the ill-will of the people amongst whom she lived ; we gather

rather from the course of the *Legend* that
her neighbours, scandalised though they may
have been, yet had some affection for her.
Pity, not resentment, met her when she returned later on to seek public forgiveness.

But, whatever may have been the attitude
of neighbours and relatives, Margaret had
already judged herself; and the energy of her
pride now passed into her repentance.   She
was not the woman to let her life flow away
in ineffectual emotion.   She had done wrong
and her life had been a scandal to her neighbours, encouraging them to sin.   She would
now confess her wrong-doing before the
world, and do penance and win pardon; that
was her duty, the duty she owed to God and
man.   She must needs leave her lover's
house, where she was no longer mistress; but
more than that, she resolved to return to his
relatives the wealth he had settled upon her
and the jewels he had given her.   Some few
ornaments she sold, and gave the price to the
poor whom she had been accustomed to help.

With the barest necessaries for herself and
her little son, she now set forth on foot
to retrace the journey of nine years before,
and return to her father's house.   It was
the instinct which so often brings the prodigal
home at last.   In the first crushed days of

repentance the days of childhood come back vividly to the prodigal's thoughts with yearning desire, and the home of his innocence becomes a vision of refuge in a world of disaster. In these days, too, the penitent is like a child, with a child's simple trust in the parent's power to shield. Bruised and shaken, the repentant, whether men or women, need the love of father or mother, or the friend who is as father or mother. The time comes when they must face the world again, and by their own resolution build up their lives anew and seek to regain a place in the society they have outraged. But it is well for them in the day of their re-birth to be shielded from the world's bitterness by the love which watches over the uncertain steps of children. The finding of this home-love is often the determining factor between a penitent's hope and despair. And so with a true instinct of nature, Margaret sought her father's house.

Yet here again we find one of those providential permissions which seem needful for the working out of Margaret's heroic story. Her father, it appears, was willing to receive her and her boy and would have taken them in ; perhaps he felt he had been already somewhat to blame. But he reckoned without his wife. She would have none of the penitent, if penitent indeed she were. The virtuous household at Laviano was no place for such as she. So Margaret was turned away from her father's door and told to go whither she would. Very simply, in words in which the tears are still undried, she herself has described the desolation and despair of that hour, in relating to her spiritual director one of those Divine intimations with which she was so often favoured after her conversion. The words are the words of Margaret, though the thought is the thought of Christ:

"Remember, *poverella*, how, thy tempter being dead, thou didst return to thy father at Laviano, with thy whole being filled with sorrow, with thy tears and drawn face, clothed in a black robe and utterly ashamed. And thy father, lacking fatherly pity, and urged on by thy stepmother, did drive thee from his house. Not knowing what to do, and being without any adviser or helper, thou didst sit down weeping under a fig-tree in his garden and there thou didst seek in Me a Guide, a Father, a Spouse and Lord; and with a humble heart didst confess thine utter misery of soul and body. Then he, the serpent of old, seeing thee cast out by thy father, sought to his own shame and thy destruction to make thy comeliness and youth an inducement to presume upon My mercy; putting it into thy heart that, since thou wast now cast out, thou mightest excusably go on in sin, and that wheresoever thou shouldst come or go thou wouldst not lack lovers amongst the great ones of the world, because of thine exceeding beauty."*

* *Leg.* i. 2.

Thus reverently is Margaret's soul unveiled to us at the supreme moment of trial. But in that hour of despair the Divine Mercy sought her out and took her by the hand and with much tenderness led her into safety. As she called upon God for help in her temptation, a voice spoke in her soul, bidding her to rise up and go to the Franciscan Friars at Cortona and put herself under their care.

It was the return of hope, and she seized upon it with the avidity of a soul utterly desolate. Yet perhaps she had some doubt as to the reception she would meet with ; for she had now tasted the bitterness of her situation, and knew by experience how the world regarded her. She does not seem to have known the Friars at Cortona, though probably she had seen some of them as they went about the country doing the work of their apostolate ; and it may be she had heard of their gentleness with sinners, a legacy bequeathed them by the Founder of the Order, who had not refused to admit a repentant robber into his fraternity. When she came to Cortona, she knew not what direction to take to get to the house of the Friars, and her evident misery and loneliness attracted the attention of two ladies whom she met when she arrived at the city. With an intuition born of pity, these ladies—Marinaria and Raneria by name—divined her trouble and spoke to her, offering to befriend her. To them Margaret told the purpose of her coming to Cortona. They immediately took her and her boy to their hearts as mothers might and gave her a home in their house. After awhile they introduced her to the Franciscan Friars, who at once extended to her a paternal pity and became to her as fathers in Christ. Thus, in the city of Cortona, Margaret found that parental solicitude which had been denied her at Laviano.

Henceforth, Cortona was her home. There she lived and developed in sanctity, till at the end she died and was buried in a church in the city. There her body has been kept these six centuries as a most priceless treasure, and there in its silver shrine it may be seen to-day, incorrupt as though this bodily incorruption were meant by Heaven to bear witness to the spiritual integrity to which she at length attained after years of contrition and penance.

*   *   *   *

It is the story of these years of purification and growing sanctity that is set forth in the *Legend* of Fra Giunta Bevegnati. The essential part of that legend will be found in this book. But first, before we speak of Fra Giunta's *Legend*, it will be well to trace the sequence of Margaret's life ; for, as we shall see, the fourteenth century Friar and friend of Margaret had no regard for chronology.

Margaret came to Cortona probably in 1273, though some would say in 1274.* The city had already acquired some fame in Franciscan history as the city of Brother Elias' predilection. Hither he had retired in the hour of his humiliation and built himself a convent and church with the generous donations of the people of Cortona, grateful to the worldly-wise Friar who had been their friend with the Emperor. He had died in their midst a sad, desolate death, just twenty years before Margaret came to give the city a holier name amongst those who loved St. Francis.

* The *Legend* gives the year 1277 as the date of Margaret's reception into the Third Order of St. Francis, and says expressly this happened three years from her conversion. P. Ludovico da Pelago, the learned editor of the *Legend*, disputes this date, assigning 1276 as the date of the Saint's reception into the Order, and 1273 as that of her conversion ; and he assumes that the date 1277 in the existing texts is an error of the copyist. But this assumption is unnecessary unless it can be proved that Fra Giunta wrote according to the Florentine style. The Pisan style seems to have been more generally used in central Italy. M. Paul Sabatier has pointed out that this style is used in all the documents concerning the Franciscan Order. (*Spec. Perfectionis*, ccxiii.) Hence, assuming that Fra Giunta used the Pisan style, any event that happened after March 25th, 1276, according to our style, would be dated 1277.

It was at the house which Elias had built that Margaret now sought renewal of life. She came in the strength of her new resolution ; but also in the weakness of her broken life. Very tenderly must she be cared for in these first days, and, indeed, for many years to come ; and this the Friars understood, as did the ladies, Marinaria and Raneria. For the first three years of her conversion the penitent knew the discouragement and seeming hopelessness of the struggle with flesh and blood. Temptation did not cease when she overcame the first impulse to despair under the fig-tree in her father's garden. Much as she abhorred her past sin, something of the old leaven still remained in her. Not that she had any desire for the former ways ; but the flesh was not yet wholly subdued by the spirit. And at times it seemed hard to her to give up all the things she had loved. Why should she embrace a penitential life and cut herself off from all worldly pleasure ? Why not be as the ordinary run of Christians ? There were days when the temptation was strong within her ; but in her innermost soul she knew it could not be. For her there must be no compromise with the world. She must be either Saint or sinner, either seek God wholly, or enjoy the world's pleasure to the full. Such was her nature ; half measures would not satisfy her.

In these struggles she found her chief earthly support in the sympathy and counsel of the Friars, particularly two, who were in a special sense her friends and directors : Fra Giovanni da Castiglione, afterwards the Custos, and Fra Giunta Bevegnati, who was also her ordinary confessor. She seems to have relied much upon Fra Giovanni, who frequently acted as her adviser until his death in 1289 ; but her chief mainstay was Fra Giunta. He was a man of intense zeal for souls and of great purity of heart ; very prudent too, and of keen sympathies. As a preacher he was simple and direct, avoiding the rhetoric so common with the preachers of the day ; on several occasions he acted as peacemaker among the citizens. To the end of her life Margaret loved to converse with him ; because of his knowledge of the soul and of Holy Scripture. And as the years went on a holy intimacy of spirit grew up between them, and the penitent became almost as much the support of the confessor in his own trials and difficulties as he was hers. But in the first year of her repentance, Fra Giunta had need of all his sympathy and tact to guide her safely through the alternation of despair and elation which came to her.

Thus, one day she came to him with a proposal of public reparation. She would go to Montepulciano, she said, garbed as a penitent and so present herself to the people who had been accustomed to see her in all her finery ; and she would hire a woman to lead her by a rope round her neck after the fashion of criminals, and the woman should call aloud as they went along : " Behold Margaret the sinner ! " But Fra Giunta would not have it, both because he thought it unbecoming in a young woman, and because he was afraid lest a singular exhibition of that sort should end in a reaction of spiritual pride. But afterwards he permitted her to go to Montepulciano and publicly beg pardon of the people one Sunday when they were assembled in the church for Mass.

Fra Giunta had, moreover, to exercise a moderating power in regard to her bodily austerities. With her excessive physical vitality, Margaret felt the need of a sharp discipline to subdue the rebellion of her body. She began to fast rigorously, abstaining altogether from flesh-meat, and contenting herself chiefly with bread and herbs. Fra Giunta on several occasions intervened, when

he thought she was overtaxing her strength ;
but Margaret's response is an indication of
the heroism of her life. " My father," she
said, " do not ask me to give hostages to this
body of mine. I cannot afford it. Between
me and my body there must needs be a
struggle until death." And Fra Giunta
understood, yet from time to time insisted
on some modification of the hard discipline
to which she would have submitted herself.

As we have seen, when Margaret turned
her back on Montepulciano, she was provided
with the barest necessaries ; and now at Cortona she began to earn her bread by nursing
the ladies of the town. But after a time she
withdrew from this sort of service, that she
might devote herself entirely to the exercise
of prayer and to the care of the sick-poor.
Thus the two tendencies which appeared
already in her life at Montepulciano now became the absorbing elements in her life : her
love of solitude and her compassion for the
wretched and suffering. The better to live
her life she withdrew from the house of the
ladies Marinaria and Raneria, and went to
live in a small cottage more secluded from
the town's traffic. Here she began definitely
to live that life of most high poverty which

St. Francis had lived at Rivo-Torto and the Portiuncula.

What that poverty was it may be well to point out, for it explains much of Margaret's story. It consisted chiefly, so far as its external manifestation went, in two things. In the first place it was an heroic dependence upon the providence of God for bodily sustenance, even so far as to the renouncing of all fixed revenues or sources of income. "Be not solicitous for your life, what you shall eat, nor for your body what you shall put on,"* was a precept of the Gospel literally accepted by St. Francis. In the second place, poverty meant to him a whole-hearted fraternising with the poor and suffering, In virtue of this chosen poverty, Francis depended for his bread upon the wages of his work, and yet more upon the alms which were given him ; for he would not even demand a definite wage for his labour. He gave his work freely, and received in return what was offered him in the way of food and clothing. If those for whom he worked either could or would not remunerate him, then he went a-begging. Indeed, much of the work done by the early Franciscans was such as would bring no wage. What wage could the lepers give ? Indeed, in

* Matthew vi. 25.

their wandering apostolic life a definite wage
could not have been earned.   The Friars,
therefore, depended chiefly upon alms for
their support.   Behind St. Francis's concep-
tion of mendicancy was the Catholic con-
ception of society as a spiritual brotherhood
in which there are no strangers, but all are
members of one family in Christ, sharing with
each other their life and goods ; the merchant
giving of his wealth, the contemplative of his
prayers, the Friar tending the lepers, and the
men at arms feeding the Friar.   It is a con-
ception of society foreign to the ultra-
individualism of Protestant Christianity, but
necessary for the right understanding of St.
Francis or of St. Margaret.

For Margaret began now to live upon alms.
Like the *Poverello* of Assisi, she went out
into the city and begged her bread ; and like
him she made it a rule only to receive the
most meagre alms, the broken bread and
leavings from the table.   The townspeople,
however, refused to see in her a common
beggar, and would insist upon giving her unbroken food.   For some time, Margaret
steadfastly refused this distinction ; she was
jealous of being the poorest of the poor,
because of Him Who had not where to lay
His Head.   But after a while a new wisdom

came to her. If people would offer her unbroken food, why not accept it and give it to
the poor who she knew were in want? So
she began to accept all that was given her,
but reserved for herself only the broken food
that remained after she had fed her needy
neighbours. At times nothing remained to
her after she had fed them, and then she herself went hungry. So, too, was it with the
clothing that was given her ; generally it went
to other poor. She received in exchange for
them their own threadbare garments. Whatever in fact came to her she considered
theirs ; and if any of them were stricken with
illness, she went and nursed them ; so that at
length they came to style her " the mother
of the poor."

There is one incident, however, in these
early days that we cannot approve so readily.
The *Legend*, undoubtedly, makes it understood that Margaret's son did not share in the
tenderness she showed to others. She seems
to have treated him with something of the
harshness with which she treated herself. Of
the alms which she received, the first share
always went to her poor neighbours, and only
when they were satisfied did her son get his
share. She told him on one occasion that in
serving the poor she knew she was serving

Christ, because she was moved by the spirit,
whereas in serving him she was not sure but
that she was obeying the impulse of the flesh.
In this statement we have doubtless the ex-
planation of her attitude towards her boy.
Her want of tenderness towards him was a
recoil from that temptation to look back upon
the past against which she had to struggle for
several long years. It may have been Fra
Giunta, with his sympathetic understanding of
her character and difficulties, who suggested
to her to send the boy to school at Arezzo.
Anyway, after awhile the boy was sent there,
and there he remained until he became a
Franciscan Friar. Later on, he was ordained
priest, and, if we may accept an intimation in
the *Legend*, he at last died a martyr's death.
There is, however, evidence that as Margaret
became more the mistress of herself and more
secure in the spiritual life, her tenderness for
her son again asserted itself. On several
occasions we find her, in the *Legend*, filled
with anxiety concerning him and coming to
his aid in difficult moments even after he was
a Friar ; for the son seems to have had a
somewhat hasty temper and not a little self-
will.

Meanwhile Margaret was reaping the reward of her stern self-discipline in a quicken-

ing of the spirit. She became ever more and more intent on prayer, and in her prayer her soul was raised up till she gazed into the mysteries of God and was drawn into a most intimate communion with her Saviour. At times she was rapt in ecstasy, as on one occasion when she was nursing a patient ; though, as her biographer tells us, she never allowed her prayer to interfere with the fulfilment of her duties towards those she served. Yet probably it was the increasing rapture of her prayer that chiefly made her give up her occupation as a nurse and seek greater solitude ; for she disliked that others should know the secret of her soul. She only wished to be thought a sinner ; she dreaded lest anyone should imagine her a Saint.

So the first three years passed away, and her bruised soul had begun to live again, and in the higher ways of the spirit she was like a child that has learned to walk and has visions of a new liberty. Temptations were still there ; even to the end, or almost to the end, she felt their presence at times. But she was conscious now of a new strength which had come to her in the recognition of a love hitherto little known to her—the love of Christ for the soul He has saved. And this love had come to her as a personal possession, a fact in her own experience ; it was not merely a word in her creed. In the presence of this new love she lived again ; timidly no doubt, because of her knowledge of herself, yet confidently too, because of the Love which had found her.

And as this love of Christ entered into her life, she began in that passionate way of hers to long for an assurance of it in some outward manifestation. She had, from her coming to Cortona, desired to be a member of the Third Order of St. Francis, but the Friars were unwilling to allow this until she had given sufficient guarantee of the sincerity of her conversion. But now Margaret, seeking, as we have said, some outward assurance, became more insistent in her request. " My fathers," she would say to them, " why do you still doubt me ? See you not that God has so strengthened me that nothing earthly can again draw me from His service ? " At length the Friars were satisfied, and Margaret was admitted a member of the Franciscan family, receiving the habit at the hands of Fra Rainaldo, the Custos of Arezzo.* This

* The Franciscan family consists of three Orders, friars, nuns (Poor Clares) and tertiaries. The genesis of these Orders is still matter of controversy. What is certain is that from A.D. 1221 these three Orders had separate organizations, though united in their spiritual descent from St. Francis. The tertiaries lived in the world and did not take claustral vows as

act put a sort of seal upon her conversion ;
at least so she regarded it.   She felt herself
no longer a spiritual waif in the Church, but
an accepted member of a spiritual family.   It
was an outward rehabilitation which gave her
an increased hope of realising the inward rehabilitation for which her soul yearned.

But an inner experience which she had
about this time conduced still more to this
confidence of which we have spoken—a confidence, be it remembered, that was ever
neighbour to a fear of her own frailty.   From
the beginning of her conversion she had been
led by a sense of God's protecting watchfulness and guidance, and as she advanced in
prayer she was drawn into very direct com-
muning with her Saviour, in which her quick-
ened soul became conscious of His words as
of the words of a near neighbour.   Of the
character of these inward communings of
Margaret with her Saviour, I shall speak
further on; here I refer chiefly to their content.

did the friars and the Poor Clares.   They did not renounce all
right of ownership ; yet they lived in great simplicity, and it
was a frequent practice amongst them to distribute to the poor
whatever property they did not need for their own support.
To appreciate fully this act, one must remember the growing
luxury of society at the time the tertiaries came into existence.
See P. Mandonnet, O.P., *Les origines de l'Ordo de Pœnitentia*
in the Report of the Fourth International Congress of Catholic
Scientists, at Friburg, 1898.   Also the same author's book :
*Les Règles et le Gouvernement de l'Ordo de Pœnitentia au
xiii. siècle.*   (Paris : Fischbacher, 1902.)

In the beginning the Divine Voice was accustomed to address her as *Poverella*, poor little one. But as the days went on and Margaret's soul more and more awakened to the spiritual life, as she came to realise Christ's love for her, she began to beseech Our Lord that He would not merely call her by a title which might be given to a stranger one pitied, but that He would address her as " My Child." It was the request of a soul that sought in the sense of a new and spiritual relationship the surest defence against the dangers of the old sinful ties. For some months, however, her request was not granted, and she was told she must first pluck out all attachment to the old life before she could effectively enter into the new life she sought. For conversion is not the work of a moment. The soul that turns away from sin does not at once cast off all attachment to its sin, and while the least attachment remains, conversion is incomplete. The penitent is as yet incapable of entering into that more intimate relationship with God, which is reserved for those whose hearts are turned wholly towards their Father's House ; though even these may feel the burden and temptations of the flesh. The "sonship of God" is not a mere sign set upon our foreheads, but the entire conversion of our being towards God so that we have no longer any attachment to sin, and the soul readily responds to the Divine intimations. This relationship is perfected when sin has no longer any power even to tempt us ; but it exists really, though inchoately, as soon as the heart's desire is wholly turned towards its Creator. Then do we begin to enter into effective communion with God as children of God. Until this comes, we are still as strangers in the house of our Father, however much we may be fostered by the Divine pity. Margaret had, therefore, to achieve entire detachment from the life she had lived, before she could enter into the effective relationship with God implied in the name she coveted.

But the day came at length when she heard the word her heart longed for ; and it came in this way. She had been praying with more insistent earnestness that this grace might be granted her, when she was told by the Inner Voice to prepare her soul by a general confession to a priest of all her sins. Whereupon she besought our Lord that her conscience might be enlightened and she might know how sinful she had been, so that her confession might be complete. And at her prayer a great light entered her soul and she stood revealed to herself in all the sins of her past life, and she saw many sins which hitherto had passed unheeded by her conscience, and therefore had not been confessed. " For the Father of mercies now manifested to her all her shame, that in the last day the just Judge might not be compelled to publish her fall to all nations and kingdoms." For eight days she went to confession to Fra Giunta, setting forth all her sins from her earliest years, "that so she might become a most pure vessel unto sanctification and honour." When her confession was finished, she went, clothed as a penitent, to receive " the Sacrament of the Body of Christ ; and having received this most living Bread which gives life to the world, she heard Jesus Christ sweetly call her His child." It was the feast of St. John the Evangelist in the year 1276, according to the most probable computation.

From this time forward Margaret's life is marked by frequent ecstasy, and as the years passed on she came more and more to live in an intimate realisation of divine mysteries. Ever more and more Christ became to her the most dominating fact in her life, and all else had for her a meaning only in reference to Him. At His feet she laid all the passionate yearning of her soul, and apart from Him she had no desire.　In very truth He became to her as " Guide and Father and Spouse and Lord ; "* and in this pure and high love she found her purification and salvation.

To the student of religious psychology, the inner life of Margaret after her conversion will be of no common interest.　For in her we have a clear illustration of the Catholic teaching that the religious life is an exaltation of man's being, not a negation ; that the Saint is one who has indeed turned aside from the ambitions and delights which satisfy the common run of men, but only to find a deeper satisfaction for both mind and heart in what is eternal.　To the multitude, eternity is nothing but the negation of time, and heaven the loss of earth.　Whereas in Catholic teaching we are told that eternity is for man the complete fulfilment of time, and heaven the substance of which earth is the shadow. We are told, too, that man is purified and saved, not so much by what he must needs deny himself, as by living the higher life in which the human becomes more spiritual in desire and achievement, less earthly in its outlook and ambition, but nevertheless not

* *Leg.* i. 2.

less human in its mode of thought and in its affections. Man must be man whether in heaven or on earth ; but the Incarnation has taught us that our human nature is capable of being wedded even with the Godhead. Not as dehumanised, therefore, can we attain to eternal life, but as purified from all that would debase our humanity below the standard set for us by our Redeemer, Christ.

To the materialist this statement of Catholic doctrine will seem but a matter of words, and the inner life of the Saint in its positive aspect nothing more than a mere idealisation of the common passions or habits of unsaintly mortals. He finds in the Saint's devotion a certain human quality, a human way of looking at and comprehending the divine, and from this he draws his conclusions. But in what other way is man to apprehend the divine life or worship save in that which is human ? Man is man, and under no circumstances can become an angelic or other substance. His worship, therefore, must needs be the consecration to the divine service of his human faculties : he must needs receive the revelation of the divine in human fashion, in forms and words that belong to human nature, else for him there would be no revelation at all. We cannot apprehend truth except through the medium of our own human experience ; we can know God only as He shows Himself to us in the reflection of our own lesser being. Yet the revelation is not the less true because it comes to us in the only fashion in which it can be intelligible to us. It only becomes the less true when we imagine that we have plumbed the whole depth of the divine life in that revelation of it which we apprehend ; for in all revelation we see the starlight, but the star itself is in the mystery of space. The revelation as it comes to us draws us closer to the divine life and increases our knowledge of God, especially in relation to ourselves. But it is necessarily limited in any particular instance by its immediate object and coloured by the human form into which it is received. With the Saints the revelation in its external form will correspond to the character of the Saint to whom it is made and to the Saint's habit of mind ; since it is only in that fashion that he can apprehend it. Further, we find that the divine revelation comes to the Saints in the earlier stages of their conversion in cruder forms of human experience than in the later stages ; and in Holy Scripture we find the same phenomenon. But this should surprise none who has stopped to examine his own apprehension of the same truth at different periods of life. A child knows what mother's love is ; yet how differently he apprehends it as he grows into youth and manhood and is able to judge of it by a fuller experience of life. How differently a painter and an engineer know the same landscape !

Returning then to the life of Margaret, we expect to find all her essential characteristics after as before her conversion. The dominant note of her character will still be her love of affection, and this will determine the character of her inner life with God. For her conversion must mean that now she will seek in God the love and sympathy her being craves, not in anything that will lead her away from God. Religion, in other words, will not take away her natural dependence upon external sympathy and affection. Margaret still remained herself, though purified and strengthened. Religion will lead her in the way of a pure love, of a love fed not by earthly passion, but by spiritual desire.

So much, Catholic teaching would lead us to expect ; and we are not disappointed. As we have said, before Margaret's salvation came to her, so soon as she recognised that Christ's love for her was a fact in life and not a mere fashion of speech, from that moment she gave herself to Him with the natural *abandon* of her character, and began to live a new life. For Margaret, one might say, the only way of salvation lay in a great love, and yet a love utterly pure and spiritual. Under other circumstances she might conceivably have found what her soul needed by way of that sacramental bond which has led many a creature to the love of the Creator. But it is safe to say that an ordinary human love would not have satisfied her. She was not of those who can drink of the measure of an earthly love, knowing its inadequacy, and rest content. The deficiency would constantly have chafed her soul. In her very need of love she was heroic, demanding an heroic measure. She was, if one may put it so, heroically *exigeante*, demanding much, yet ready to give much in return, even her very self. Even in the days of her sin she had been loyal to her lover, and would have scorned the treachery of lesser souls ; though it is evident her soul hungered for more than her lover could give her, and that a certain desolateness made her seek solitary places, and dream of another life. But the love of Christ came home to her as that which she needed—at once measureless and utterly pure ; and from the day that she realised Christ as a living presence, she lived, like Magdalene, at His feet. Not otherwise could she have lived and been saved.

One day—it was the same day on which Christ had first addressed her as " My child " —Fra Rainaldo, the Custos, put this question to her : " Supposing there were a poor soul burdened with sin, and thou by renouncing Christ's presence couldst save that soul, what wouldst thou do ? "* Margaret was much troubled. Willingly, she said, would she do aught to save a soul, yet she well knew that without Christ's presence she could not live. For her this presence was a necessity, if her life was not to close up into itself like the flowers which close at nightfall. She could not live save in the warmth and light of Him whom her soul loved. That was her character reproduced in her spiritual experience.

It is not for lesser souls to know all that this presence of Christ means to the soul who realises it as the sunlight of daily consciousness.

> " Jesu, spes pœnitentibus,
> Quam pius es petentibus,
> Quam bonus te quaerentibus,
> Sed quid invenientibus ! "

* *Leg.* vii. 22.

To such as Margaret this presence is more
vivid than things of sense. Not that they
realise it at all times with the same mental
distinctness. Nay, there are days when
Christ seems lost to them, and they pass
through a desolation as of Holy Saturday.
Nevertheless, once they have realised this
presence, their life becomes dominated by it,
and they live thenceforth in its enjoyment, or
in its expectation, or in a sense of its loss ;
except, perhaps, in moments of distraction,
when the spiritual sense becomes numbed by
secular cares. So was it with Margaret almost
from the beginning of her conversion. To
her, Christ was verily the living Christ, even
as He was to Magdalene on the morning of
the resurrection ; and, having realised His presence, she was lifted above the shadows in
which hitherto she had sought her soul's desire.

It may be said that Margaret's love of
Christ had in it something of an earthly
quality, more especially at first ; that she
sought in Christ's presence a certain sensible
delight. In the *Legend* we undoubtedly hear
from time to time an echo of the *noli Me
tangere* of the Gospel. But that is only to
say that Margaret did not at one bound attain
to an entirely spiritual intuition and affection,
and that at first she apprehended Christ's

presence through the imperfect medium of an understanding not yet freed from the forms and measures of earth.   In its most absolute submission to earth-forms and measures the human mind cannot regard Christ as other than mere man passed into the grave of history.   The realisation that Christ is still living indicates the mind's emancipation from earth-measures ; yet from this to the perfect apprehension of the heavenly Christ runs the entire gamut of the spiritual life.   Many of those who recognise the living Christ never in this world realise more of Him than can be seen from the gateway of those ordinary experiences which come to us in our relations with the things of earth.   He comes to us clothed in the form of our own purer and more spiritual experience.   We are led onwards, if we are eager enough, to greater spirituality, and as we become more spiritual in ourselves, so does our apprehension of Christ become more spiritual.   Yet we must needs pass, as St. Bernard might put it, through the way of the flesh, gradually freeing ourselves from its crudities and limitations, until we stand revealed in the fulness of the spirit.   In other words, we must needs begin in an imperfect spirituality that we may pass into that which is more perfect.

Margaret, realising in her life the presence of the living Christ, and won by its beauty, at once gave herself to its worship with a whole-hearted devotion. She gave herself as she was, an imperfect creature seeking the highest, but as yet far from it. Her initial heroism and sanctity lay not in what she achieved, but in the entire devotion with which she sought her Lord and His ways. So Magdalene, yet imperfect in the spiritual life, was a Saint in the complete sincerity of her " Rabboni ! "

How Margaret's love for Christ purified her soul and wrought in it all manner of heroism, is taught in Fra Giunta's *Legend*. Nor will we here venture to do more than indicate some of the main points of contact between her inner experience and that of the great wide world, so that those who read the *Legend* may the more easily gather its fruit. At the outset our sympathy is won to this heroic soul by the naïve revelation of the weakness of her character in the midst of its great strength. Margaret the Saint is very much Margaret the woman, and the woman who needs affection and the demonstration of affection. There is something of the spoilt child in her longing for spiritual favours ; she is easily elated by the presence of Christ, and as easily

depressed when His presence is withdrawn.
Not once only did our Lord rebuke her for
this fault.

"Margaret," He would say to her, "thou dost
seek to have Heaven even here on earth : bear in
mind that this cannot be. Life on earth is for toil
and temptation ; and if at times I grant the consolation of My presence, thou must not yet forget that
thou must also at times walk in darkness and suffer."

And once He rebuked her, saying :

"Why art thou so full of thyself, seeking thine
own enjoyment in My presence, when thou shouldst
be thinking of thy neighbours, praying and working
for their souls."

And listen to this from Fra Giunta :

"Now Margaret, though she desired that all men
should be pleasing in God's sight, yet wished that
she should be favoured more than others."

It was a human weakness which brought
her a lesson on the selflessness of perfect
charity. Even her humility was not always
dissociated from a self-consciousness which
was blameable, and drew upon her our Lord's
rebuke.*

Yet we do not revere Margaret any the
less because we find her thus, even in her
saintly ways, a very woman of human imperfection which declares her sister to common
humanity. On the contrary, it is good for us

* *Leg.* vi. 25.

to learn that the divine ways are open to mortals not yet perfect, though of good-will. And it is good, too, to learn how the Divine Wisdom accommodates itself to our weakness. The *Legend* tells us that in her later years Margaret was less favoured with sensible sweetness in her communings with Heaven than she had been in the beginning, and that Christ led her by a higher way, a more intimate communion of spirit, in which outward and sensible manifestation had less part.*

In the earlier years she was as one who needs frequent assurances and gifts to strengthen her faith in the love which surrounds her, and who sees in the absence of such assurances the withdrawal of love itself. Afterwards her faith became stronger, so that outward assurances were no longer needful. She entered into that intimate understanding which can dispense with external words and signs. But for many years Margaret was very dependent upon the sensible sweetness of her Saviour's presence. It was as a healing to her bruised soul in her struggles with temptation. For, as we have said, Margaret was tempted to the very end ; and because of this she lived in a perpetual fear lest, in spite

* *Leg.* viii. 15.

of the heavenly favours granted her, she might fail. The spirit was willing, but the flesh was still somewhat weak. And the very intensity with which she lived her spiritual life subjected her at moments of physical reaction to the stronger temptation ; for temptation is often the backwash of the energy which has just accomplished some spiritual purpose, and carried the soul to some spiritual goal. That is why, until the domination of the soul is secured, the Saints are not infrequently subject to temptation fiercer than that known to ordinary mortals. Hence, too, in their keenest spiritual experiences, wise souls are on their guard against the temptation to follow ; and this explains the need of discipline and austerity which enters so largely into a Saint's life long after he has attained to exalted sanctity.

It was with the wisdom of experience, therefore, that when Fra Giunta was counselling Margaret to mitigate her austerities, she replied : " My father, until death I must needs make no compromise with my body."* The very character of her spiritual life demanded more than ordinary watchfulness, lest the flesh should rob the spirit of its glory.

So, during the twenty-three years of her

* *Leg.* iii. 7.

conversion, Margaret's inner life is a constant passing from ecstasy to temptation, and from temptation to ecstasy. At one moment she gazes into the mysteries of Heaven, and her soul is inundated with the joy of Paradise ; at another, the glory has passed, and she feels herself a " clod of earth."   Now it is Thabor, and again it is the angry sea and Peter crying out : " Lord, save me or I perish."   But ever and anon, as the temptation is conquered, Christ the Consoler comes to her, and strengthens her with the joy of His presence.

After a time Margaret got to know the value of temptation as a factor in the building up of the spiritual life. At first she was inclined to complain. It seemed to her that in the strife with evil no good could come to her, but only the taint of sin. " Lord, I cannot believe such suffering as this can benefit my soul," she replied, one day, when Christ told her that in such suffering her soul would be cleansed.* She had not then learnt that in conquering temptation man attains to a maturity of spirit which enables him to enter more deeply into communion with the divine life. But in time she learned the lesson, and though the knowledge took away nothing

* *Leg.* v. 29.

from the bitterness of the struggle, it yet gave her greater resignation in accepting it.

But the mystery of Margaret's purification reaches its ultimate poignancy in her self-judgment: that self-judgment through which all men must pass either for salvation or despair, either in life or in death. The Saints have their judgment in this life, when for the first time they come, as it were, face to face with the sanctity of God. The self-judgment of the soul in the moment of death has been nobly described by Cardinal Newman in his " Dream of Gerontius." The soul is brought, whilst yet the priest and mourners are uttering the *Subvenite*, to "the dear feet of Emmanuel," and, in the presence of the speckless purity of its Judge, judges itself in those sad sweet lines :

" Take me away and in the lowest deep
    There let me be,
And there in hope the lone night watches keep,
    Told out to me.
There motionless and happy in my pain,
    Lone not forlorn,
There will I sing my sad perpetual strain,
    Until the morn."

The judgment of the soul awakened in this life to the vision of God's holiness has much the same effect of self-abasement. It is then that the soul realises what sin is, and instinctively shrinks back from the Divine presence.

In the history of Margaret's inner life we constantly find her joy in the presence of her Saviour passing into wonderment at the infinite mercy which can deign to look upon so vile a creature; and it was surely a miracle of love that kept her willingly in the Divine presence. At times her self-abasement finds expression in words which seem an exaggeration of fact. " Lord," she cries, "how canst Thou speak with me who am the vilest of creatures, for verily I believe no creature is, or ever was, so vile as I am!" But the exaggeration disappears when we remember that Margaret is judging herself in the light of the divine purity which has shone into her soul and revealed her to herself. With this divine purity beating upon her own imperfection, she is appalled by her own unworthiness, and sincerely believes no other creature can be as wanting in goodness as she. Their sin is hidden from her in the shadow of their own souls; her sin stands revealed in the light of the divine holiness. So again, as she comes to see more deeply into the divine life, her self-abasement increases until she wonders that God can let her live.

Yet this self-abasement of the Saint has in it nothing of morbid introspection or torturing self-analysis : for the Saint's eye is turned not so much on self as on the divine Exemplar. She is abashed before the infinite purity which she worships, and in which she finds her delight. She yearns with an infinite yearning to approach nearer to the sanctuary. She does not lose her soul in inarticulate longings and purposeless self-questioning. In her self-abasement is a great hope—the hope of that ultimate purification which her soul desires. For in the Divine holiness she has discovered the infinite love which seeks out and saves the penitent, however great his sins may have been. In the recognition of this infinite love Margaret regained herself and her own self-reverence. If God so holy can love her, why should she despair of herself ? For God's sake she must strive to regain her innocence, and so justify His love of her. With the repentant queen of the " Idylls of the King," she might say :

" I must not scorn myself ; He loves me still."

With this knowledge of God's enduring love it was that Margaret set herself to live down her sin, and prepare herself for " the world where all are pure." In hope and self-

reverence she began her new life : in innocence she completed it. Meanwhile, however,
it is pathetic to find her, in the midst of Divine
favours, overwhelmed with the sense of her
own unworthiness.   One day Christ remon-
strated with her.   " Can I not dispense My
favours," He said, " to whomsoever I please ?
Hast thou forgotten Magdalene and the
Samaritan woman, and the Canaanite, and
Matthew the tax-gatherer whom I chose to
be My Apostle, and the thief to whom I
promised Paradise ? "   But Margaret replied :
" Yea, Lord, I remember ; yet even so I do
not think they were so destitute of virtue as I
am."

Thus in temptation and self-abasement was
Margaret purified and strengthened, whilst
she drew ever nearer in mind and heart to
Christ, her Lord.   As the years went on she
grew in spiritual stature ; and the days, as
they brought her an assurance of forgiveness,
took from her that something of self-hatred
and hardness which obtruded itself in the first
years of her conversion.   To the end she
sorrowed for the past, but it was with a
gentler sorrow, which had in it some of
the mystery of the Saviour's love.   And
indeed the love of her Lord gradually
absorbed all other emotions within her until

these became mere incidents in the way. Of Margaret might have been written these verses of the early Franciscan poet :

> " In Christo e nata nova creatura,
> Spogliato homo vecchio e fato novello ;
> Ma tanto amore monta cum ardura,
> Lo cor par che se fenda cum coltello,
> Mente cum senno tolle tal calura
> Christo se me tra tutto tanto bello."*

But Margaret was no mere recluse. Were it not for the revelation of her inner life left us by Fra Giunta, she might be chiefly remembered in the annals of her adopted town as the foundress of Cortona's great hospital and of an association of Mercy ; or perhaps as one of those women not infrequently met with in the history of medieval Europe, women who were true mothers of their country, as were Judith and Deborah amongst the people of Israel. St. Catherine of Siena and Jeanne d'Arc have world-wide fame ; but many an Italian city and province had its Rose of Viterbo—the girl Saint who died at eighteen, after preaching a successful crusade against the tyrant Emperor.

* I venture the following translation :

> " In Christ mankind is born again,
> The old cast out, the new shall reign ;
> But oh ! so fierce a love is mine,
> My heart by love is rent in twain,
> And all my thoughts to Him incline :
> Christ the All-Beautiful, I am Thine."

With these Margaret claims a place,
because of her frequent interventions for peace
in the wars and feuds of Cortona.   Hardly
had she taken the habit of a penitent of St.
Francis when she received a command in
prayer to send word to the Bishop of Arezzo,
the diocesan of Cortona, and bid him amend
his ways, and cease carrying on war with the
people of his own diocese and of the neighbouring cities.   This command came to her
in 1277, on May 5th.   A few days later she
was commanded to repeat her warning, and
to tell the Bishop that, unless he heeded her
words now, the hour would come when he
would himself seek mercy, and not find it.   It
required some courage to upbraid Bishop
Guglielmo Ubertini Pazzi ; and it may be
that the second command came to Margaret
because of hesitation on her part in carrying
out the commission of May 5th.   For Guglielmo Ubertini was no meek-hearted priest,
but a soldier prelate, like that Bishop of
Beauvais who fell into the hands of Richard
Cœur-de-Lion.   He had been put into the
bishopric of Arezzo by the Emperor Frederic
II. in defiance of the Pope, after the murder
of Bishop Marcellino, who had been a faithful
upholder of the rights of the Holy See.
Alexander IV., in 1256, had, however, for the

sake of peace, acknowledged Guglielmo as prince-bishop. To the Bishop the temporalities of his See were of more concern than the souls of his people; and he spent the years of his episcopate either in wars or in intrigue. As is not uncommonly the case, he seems to have united a certain superstitious reliance upon the prayers of others with the lawlessness of his own life.* This, perhaps, made him listen to Margaret; for two months later we find him concluding peace with the people of Cortona.

Two years after this, in 1279, Tuscany was again on the point of becoming a theatre of war. This time the quarrel was between Charles of Anjou, King of Sicily, and the German Emperor, Rudolph of Hapsburg, each contending for the protectorate of central Italy. The French troops were already assembling in the marches of Ancona, when the people of Cortona, dreading invasion, came to Margaret and besought her to pray that war might be averted. Margaret prayed, and, in the intensity of her desire, offered herself a victim to appease the Divine anger, if only the people might be saved: for to her it seemed that these wars were a punishment permitted by Heaven because of the sins of

* *Leg.* ix. 45.

the time.   And as she prayed it was revealed
to her that an armistice had already been
arranged between the contending parties ;
and so the townsfolk of Cortona rejoiced.   In
a short while a satisfactory peace was
established through the intervention of the
Pope.

There was yet another instance of Margaret's endeavour to stave off war in 1289.
Guglielmo, the Bishop, was again in arms
against the Guelphs.   Margaret, by divine
command, went to him, and besought him as
a prelate of the Church to desist.   But now
he would not listen to her.   Ten days later,
on June 11th, he was killed in battle, whilst
charging the enemy in the plains of Bibbiena.
The Florentines, in mockery, took his helmet
and sword, and hung them up in the Church
of St. John, in Florence.   And thus Guglielmo
Ubertini passed away.   Yet, thanks to Margaret's influence, the Cortonese had reason to
remember the unhappy Bishop not wholly as a
tyrant ; for to him they owed in some measure
the incorporation of the hospital, and the
nursing sisterhood and confraternity of Mercy
which she founded.

It was in 1286 that the Bishop granted the
charter which crowned the Saint's endeavour
to relieve the misery of the sick poor of

Cortona. It will be recalled how, in the first days of her conversion, Margaret earned her bread by nursing the ladies of the city, and how, after a time, she retired from their service that she might be free at once to pray more in seclusion, and to tend the poor. At first she must have attended them in their own homes ; but soon her cottage became the centre whither the poor came to take all their miseries of soul and body. After a while other pious women associated themselves with her in her work of mercy. Of these, three are named in the *Legend*, Gilia and Adriana, whose souls Margaret was afterwards assured had found a place among the blessed—for they died before Margaret— and another Margaret, apparently a native of Siena, a rare soul (the *Legend* tells us) in whom God took especial delight. Then there was a lady, Diabella, who took particular interest in the work, and eventually gave Margaret a house for the sick ; and this was the beginning of the hospital.

For Margaret now thought it time to put her work upon a more secure basis, and to make the city responsible for the care of its sick poor. In this project she had the sympathy and practical assistance of the chief citizen of Cortona, Uguccio Casali, elected

Podesta of the city in 1280.   Uguccio Casali
was a hero with the Cortonese.   "Uguccio
il grande," they styled him ; and deservedly
so, for he had headed the party of independ-
ence against the Bishop of Arezzo, and had
been the hope of the citizens in the dark days
before Margaret gained the Bishop's ear.
Probably he was grateful for her intervention.
At his instance the City Council promised
support ; and thus in 1286 the Hospital of
our Lady of Mercy—Spedale di S. Maria della
Misericordia—was opened.   The nursing
Sisters attached to the hospital were tertiaries
of St. Francis, whom Margaret formed into a
congregation with special statutes.   The Cortonese styled them *le poverelle*—the little
poor ladies.   This congregation was one of
the earliest of those Franciscan sisterhoods
which, under the rule of the Third Order,
devoted themselves to the service of the poor,
anticipating by nearly four centuries the work
of St. Vincent de Paul.   They were unenclosed,
and carried on their work much as the active
sisterhoods do now, until the Council of Trent
decreed that all nuns should be bound to
enclosure, a regulation, demanded, doubtless,
by the circumstances of the times, which was
so soon to be modified in practice by the
Sisters of Charity and the host of modern

sisterhoods.   The *poverelle* existed at Cortona until their dispersion in the Napoleonic revolution.   They were never restored ; but their convent was in 1820 taken over by Visitation nuns.

But besides the hospital and the *poverelle*, there was the confraternity of our Lady of Mercy, which Margaret instituted with the approval of Bishop Guglielmo.   The members of this confraternity, who were drawn from all the families of Cortona, bound themselves in the first place to support the hospital ; but beyond this their charity was to embrace the needy, wherever found, and more particularly the respectable poor who were ashamed to beg.   And, that the assistance might be the more sure, the associates were themselves to go round seeking out the poor and investigating their needs.   They were to place their brains and sympathy at the service of the indigent, as well as their purses.   Besides this, the confraternity undertook to assist poor monasteries and convents, and to help prisoners who were without means to defend their cause.   Moreover, in case of civil war, the associates were to make every effort to bring about peace.

Thus Margaret repaid the city of Cortona for its adoption of the outcast penitent.   Yet these public achievements, bearing witness as they do to the genius of the woman, as well as to the virtue of the Saint, did not exhaust her pitying thoughtfulness for her fellow men. There was no sorrow she did not sympathise with, and strive to alleviate, once it was made known to her, and this in spite of a constant longing for solitude. She became, in fact, prophetess and healer to Cortona and the surrounding country. To her came the distressed and the diseased seeking relief. If a child were sick, the parents would come to Margaret that she might lay her hands on the sick, and bring back health. Those who were strongly tempted to sin would come laying bare their temptation, and seeking in her prayers and words of counsel the moral strength they lacked. If a mother despaired of a son's salvation, because of his evil life, she came begging of Margaret to send him some bread from her table, believing that if the son but tasted bread sanctified by Margaret's presence he would be converted. So the stream of petitions went on unceasingly. It was useless for Margaret to plead that she was a sinner like themselves, and that because of her sins her very touch would soil them. The people disbelieved her protestations, and believed the more in the efficacy of her inter-

And it was not only the affairs of the Cortonese, public or private, that appealed to Margaret. Both in the ecclesiastical and in the civil world the times were in a turmoil, and in every city the events of the far-off world found an echo, causing hope or consternation, or giving matter for gossip. Such echoes from the larger world are found in Margaret's story. At one time it is the crusade which Pope Nicholas IV endeavoured to raise against the increasingly victorious Turk. One by one the Christian strongholds in the East were falling, when the Pope, in an encyclical letter, dated January 5th, 1290, called once more on all Christian princes to make peace amongst themselves, and to turn their arms against the desecrater of the Holy Places. A Franciscan Friar himself, Nicholas IV. commissioned the Franciscans especially to preach the holy war, and to collect money for carrying it through. But the day for a crusade was gone. The mystical devotion to the Sacred Humanity of Christ which, blended with a thirst for adventure, had made the crusades of the eleventh and twelfth centuries possible, was dying out. The crusading spirit had really expired before the walls of Damietta. Yet there were many devout souls who still yearned to see the Holy Places in Christian custody; and the crusade was still part of the official policy of the Holy See, face to face with the disintegration of the mediæval system. Margaret, in her passionate love of the Saviour, was all on fire with enthusiasm for the new crusade. She not only urged the Friars to fulfil their commission with all diligence, but herself pleaded with the Cortonese to support the project generously. The failure of the scheme must have been to her a sore disappointment.

Then again, in 1295, devout souls in Italy were not a little agitated by a sentence of excommunication fulminated by a certain Bishop in Italy against those who should visit the chapel of the Portiuncula at Assisi with the purpose of gaining the traditional Indulgence attached to the chapel: which Indulgence, said the Bishop, had been annulled by the Fourth Council of Lateran, even supposing it had ever been valid. At once the Franciscans were up in arms for the honour of the chapel St. Francis loved so well; and, in the end, the famous Indulgence was vindicated, and its validity assured by the Holy See. But for a time there was perturbation of spirit amongst the devout in all Italy; for the Indulgence was much prized. Margaret's sympathies were touched, for one of her companions at the hospital had just died after making a visit to the Portiuncula ; but she was comforted by an assurance in prayer that the excommunication would be withdrawn, and that Sister Adriana, the dead companion, had entered into eternal glory through having gained the indulgence.*

Thus, now with Martha now with Mary, Margaret served Christ her Lord. But ever as the days went on she thirsted more and more for the eternal home where no shadows veil the Divine Presence from the eyes of man. Often with a gentle vehemence did she protest against the days that kept her from that unveiled Presence, and pray that the time might be hastened ; and when she was told that this might not be until the measure of her probation was fulfilled, she would beseech the Lord that she might at least retire into solitude, and live her life in contemplation at His feet even here on earth. But the heavenly Voice replied : "Not for thyself alone art thou specially favoured with

* *Leg.* ix. 34, 49, 50. This reference to the Pardon of Assisi, as the Indulgence is called, is noteworthy, since there are but few references to the Indulgence in Franciscan literature previous to the attestation of Theobald, Bishop of Assisi, about A.D. 1310. See Sabatier, *Tractatus de Indulgentia S. M. de Portiuncula.*

My Grace, but for the sake of others, too, that through thee they may learn of the Divine Mercy." And again the Voice said to her: "Margaret, think not of thyself alone, but of thy neighbours, for whose sake I suffered." And so the heart-longing would be repressed, and Margaret would continue to work and toil for the citizens of Cortona and all who came to her.

In truth, she followed her Saviour in His ministry amongst men, even as her spiritual leader St. Francis had followed. In poverty, in service of the poor, in sorrowing, and in contemplation of the Divine Mercy, she lived her life and drew ever nearer to Him Whom her soul loved. And as her love deepened, she wished to spend herself in sacrifice, even as He had, for the souls He came to redeem. Passionately she would weep at times at the thought of the sufferings of Christ, especially in His last hours. To her the drama of Galilee and Calvary was an ever-present reality, stretching out until the end of time. Christ still lived for souls, still wandered the earth seeking them, still knew hunger and fatigue on His journey, was still rebuffed, still suffered and died. At times these mysteries became to her so vivid and real that she lost consciousness of the transitory present, and was wholly absorbed in the spiritual drama which was her life : this was particularly the case in Holy Week, when in the Church the story of the Great Pasch is re-enacted in solemn office and ritual, and so vividly portrayed that even ordinary mortals sharing in the service are carried across the centuries, and for a fleeting hour or so are taken into the very life of the Passion. To Margaret all this was a very reality in her own spiritual life, and produced in her an intense desire to suffer as Christ suffered, and to sacrifice herself for souls even as He sacrificed Himself.

And in many ways she had to suffer throughout her days, as I have already observed in telling the story of her conversion. But the martyrdom of the spirit which she suffered was made complete by the suffering inflicted on her by the ill-nature of some amongst the Cortonese who in general loved her so well ; so that she shared in the Passion of her Saviour even to being reviled and suspected of evil. From the beginning there were those who doubted her sincerity ; nor is it surprising that there should have been prophets of evil when the penitent was young and of great beauty. But long after she had given heroic proofs of her conversion the evil-speaking tongues continued to wag.

The bitterest moment came to Margaret when suspicion was cast upon the singleness of her relations with Fra Giunta.   He had been accustomed to visit her very frequently, because he knew her need of sympathy and encouragement in the ceaseless struggle she had to wage against the temptation to despair; and because he knew, too, the narrow path along which her course lay, and the many dangers which beset a soul called by God to walk along unfrequented paths in the spiritual life.

Even the Friars, her friends, were affected by the gossip, and Fra Giunta was forbidden to visit her more than once a week, except when she was seriously ill.   The Friars at least, Margaret thought, might have spared her the humiliation, since Christ had Himself committed her to their charge.   And then further misunderstandings occurred which strained the relations between Margaret and the Friars, and resulted, in 1289, in Fra Giunta being removed from Cortona and sent to Siena.   The year previous to this Margaret had removed her dwelling from the Hospital to a house on the outskirts of the city.   This she did by a Divine command.   But the Friars opposed the change, chiefly because they did not wish her to go

so far away from their church. Already her
health was broken, and probably she would
not live many years ; and they who had
charge of her in life wished, as Fra Giunta
puts it, to have the custody of her body
after death. Twice Margaret deferred to
their wishes. A third time, however, the
Divine Voice charged her to obey God
rather than man. "Tell the Friars Minor,"
said Christ to her, "that, though I have
committed thee to their charge, yet I Myself
am thy first Guide and Master." But, to
console them, she was to tell the Friars that
after her death they would assuredly have the
custody of her body. They were, however,
hardly satisfied. After this third intimation
from heaven Margaret went to her new dwelling. The following year, in the Chapter of
the Order held at Siena, Fra Giunta was taken
away, and a new director appointed for her,
Fra Filippo, the newly-elected Custos of
Arezzo. During the Chapter Margaret had
been warned in prayer of the decision of the
Capitular Fathers, and had sent for Fra
Giunta and told him what had happened.
Then, in great distress, she sought courage in
prayer, and it was revealed to her that her
faithful guide should again return to Cortona
and be with her at her death. And so it

happened : for Fra Giunta remained at Siena seven years, and was then sent back to Cortona the year before Margaret died. Yet during those seven years these two souls, who understood each other so well, were not entirely separated ; letters passed between them, and on several occasions Fra Giunta paid a visit to Cortona at Margaret's request, in order to make peace between contending families.

The Divine command that she should change her dwelling was a concession to Margaret's longing for greater solitude ; but it might almost be said that she was sent to prepare for herself her future shrine. The house she inhabited adjoined the Church of St. Basil, no longer used for public worship since it had been sacked a few years previously by the soldiers of the Prince-Bishop of Arezzo. In Margaret the sight of a ruined church would cause the same feeling of outrage as it caused in St. Francis, who with his own hands repaired the churches in and near Assisi which were falling into ruins. Margaret had the Church of St. Basil restored, and in 1290 Hildebrand, the new Bishop of Arezzo, opened it for public worship, appointing Ser Badia Ventura chaplain, much to Ser Badia's spiritual benefit, for when he came there he was not over-careful of the dignity of the Divine service, nor did a sense of his priestly obligations weigh on his soul. There was, however, no great evil in him, and under Margaret's tuition he became a zealous, saintly priest. "My son Badia," she styles him in the *Legend.*

But at length the time came when Margaret's earthly struggle was over. The day had been arduous and wearying, and she welcomed the evening as it drew in, bringing a foretaste of the eternal peace. Her great vitality had borne her up under austerities and the long stress of inward combat, but at length her bodily powers began to fail her, and she knew the end was nigh. Fra Giunta had come back to Cortona, as the Divine Voice had promised, and his understanding sympathy, which had strengthened her in many an hour of trial, now comforted her in these last days, when heaven seemed so near, and yet—for who is pure when God is at hand?—might even now be lost.

Whatever fear might cross her soul, Margaret remembered the promise given her some years before. One day when she was in prayer she had in a vision seen St. Mary Magdalene in the midst of the virgins at the throne of God ; and as she wondered at this, it was revealed to her that Magdalene by her repentance had attained again to the state of virginal innocence. At the same time she was assured that she, too, would one day be placed amongst the virgins in heaven. In the strength of that promise, Margaret had lived and striven and conquered, and now the goal was in sight.

Candlemas Day came in the year 1297, bringing to her watching soul a strange joy as she listened in spirit to the *Nunc Dimittis* echoing through the Christian world, proclaiming how holy Simeon had waited and had beheld at last. And Margaret listened with a great content, for she already knew that for her, too, the Light of the World was fast approaching. Three days later she fell into a state of great weakness, and from that time she was unable to take any food. On February 22, just before daybreak, she passed joyously away. It was twenty-three years since her conversion.

Immediately the popular voice of Cortona proclaimed her a Saint. The Franciscans, naturally enough, desired that she should be buried in the Church of St. Francis, whither she had come seeking guidance when cast out of her father's house. But the city determined her body should rest in the Church of St. Basil, which she had caused to be restored. And so she was buried there, with solemn pomp. Nine years later, Hildebrand, the Bishop who had authorised the re-opening of the church at Margaret's request, determined to rebuild it. On June 21 he issued a letter to all the faithful, appealing for funds to restore the church, "in which rests the body of the blessed Margaret, by whose merits many miracles shine forth in this same place; where also the Brethren of Penance dwell." This last sentence can only mean that there was a congregation of tertiaries attached to the church, for it was served by secular chaplains until 1385. Then some Olivetan monks took charge of the shrine, but they abandoned it after five years, and for a while the church was again desolate. But in 1392 the city council made it over to the care of the Friars Minor, with the prayer that henceforth in this church the blessed Margaret "would lovingly and graciously be ready to extend helping hands to all who had recourse to her," and "keep the peace both within and without the city."

At last the Friars had entered into the fulfilment of Margaret's promise that after her death they should have the custody of her body.   Doubtless the delay was not due merely to unwillingness on the part of the city.   The Friars at Cortona had passed through some unedifying vicissitudes during the closing years of the Saint's life.   The Fraticelli, fanatical zealots of the Waldensian, rather than of the Franciscan, type, had intruded themselves into the *Celle* on the outskirts of Cortona, where St. Francis is said to have written his Testament ; and thus the disputes, which at that time were threatening to shatter the Order of Friars Minor were brought into Cortona.   Moreover, these Fraticelli had shown but little reverence for the penitent at St. Basil's ; and, in the shifting conditions of the times, it was not impossible that the Church of St. Francis in the city would fall into their hands.   Fra Giunta and the Friars who had had the care for so many years of Margaret's soul were grievously disappointed.   Again and again does Fra Giunta repeat in his *Legend* that Christ Himself committed Margaret to the charge of the Friars Minor ; it was his protest against the detention of her body at St. Basil's.   Could he have foreseen the day when this church would be dedicated to Margaret, and served by the Friars, his soul might have been content.   As it was, he lived to see the church become a shrine whither crowds came to seek relief in spiritual and temporal need, encouraged by the Bishops in many parts of Italy, who freely bestowed Indulgences on the pilgrims and those who contributed to the building of the new church.* And perhaps it was in reply to the continued protest of the Friars that Bishop Hildebrand added those words to his letter of appeal for funds : " Where also the Brethren of Penance dwell."

Margaret, acclaimed a Saint by the popular voice on the day of her death, and invoked by Bishops and Popes throughout the centuries that followed, was not formally canonised until May 16, 1728. But for two centuries previous to this her festival had been annually celebrated, with the Pope's sanction, in the diocese of Cortona and by the Franciscan Orders.

*　　　　*　　　　*　　　　*

The original *Legend* was written by Fra Giunta Bevegnati,† the Saint's confessor,

---

* Fra Giunta was alive in A.D. 1318, as is witnessed by a will drawn up in that year, wherein it is directed that certain alms are to be distributed with the advice of Fra Giunta, if he should be living at the death of the testator. See P. Ludovico da Pelago, *Dissert.* iv.

† The Bevegnati were inhabitants of Cortona who came from Pisa in the early part of the thirteenth century. See P. Ludovico da Pelago, *Dissert.* iv.

and was finished by 1308, in which year it was solemnly approved by the Pope's Legate, Cardinal Napoleone Orsini.

Fra Giunta wrote what he had heard from Margaret's own lips, and from those who shared with him the care of her soul ; and at the end he compiled from his notes a " legend," in which he sets forth all that he knew of the penitent's story—or, at least, all that he thought the world ought to know. In this *Legend*, as in most mediæval legends, there is no chronological sequence ; facts which happened in the early days of Margaret's life at Cortona are set down side by side with facts which belong to her later years.   Fra Giunta's idea was to group together the various incidents of his penitent's life according as they illustrate certain points in her character.   Thus, one chapter illustrates her humility ; another chapter her devotion to the Passion of Christ ; a third chapter tells us of her compassion for the poor, and so forth.   Often the incidents related are very similar in character and detail, and the reading is apt at times to become wearisome.

But when we disentangle the essential narrative from the prolixities which overburden it, we have a record throbbing with

life.   It is, in truth, Margaret's story told in
her own words, and in the intimate confidence which existed between her and her
spiritual guide.   Only with reluctance, and as
compelled by a will to which her own must
bow, did she thus reveal the workings of her
soul, knowing that Fra Giunta would use
her confidences for the good of other
souls.   Sometimes she would plead : " Lord,
why may I not guard the secret of the
King ? " and the answer given would be :
" Because it is not for thyself alone these
things are done in thee, but for the sake of
all who sin, that through thee they may learn
the vastness of My mercy."   And so, under
a heavenly compulsion, she related the
wonders that were wrought in her.   But to
the end this self-revelation remained to her a
great trouble.   It troubled her to be set up
as a sign to others, she who never lost the
sense of her own unworthiness.   At times it
was a burden almost too hard to be borne,
a mockery of her own life ; only that it was
the command of Him who cannot mock.
And this threw her back again on the
mystery of God's mercy, and she submitted
in all humility ; for how could she hold out
against her Saviour ?

Yet, if to-day we are able to gaze into the

inner recesses of her soul, and witness the process of her spiritual restoration, let us remember that we do so at the cost of great anguish on the part of Margaret. This was no Marie Bashkirtshef, clamorous for the world's notice and pity ; but one set up against her will as a sign to others. We read this record of a soul's experience, knowing that it comes to us as a message from heaven ; and yet it is an intensely human document. It is a human soul that is bared to us ; and a woman's soul whose heart-strings are attuned with exquisite sensitiveness to every human emotion, and, touched by the spirit of life, give forth a searching melody of joy and pain, of ecstasy and desolation, of eager desire and utter diffidence. And it is no uncertain melody, for every note pulsates with definite, vital experience. Margaret was of those who live in every moment of their existence, and who, for good or for evil, are, by a sort of natural destiny, a power among their fellows.

But Margaret is not only throughout her life a very woman, she is also a woman of Italy. She comes before us in all the passionateness of the Italian nature, which expresses itself with emphasis and superlatives, where we of the North would speak with reserve and in the degree positive. It is necessary to bear this in mind if we would understand Margaret aright. But beneath the racial temperament there is always present the essential human note to which human nature, whether of the North or South, will surely respond. The style of the language is that of Italy, but the words flow direct from a woman's heart.

Some there are, doubtless, who would object that the colloquies between Margaret and her Saviour are but a woman's fond imaginings. Even were this so, these self-revelations would be worthy of reverence, as setting forth the aspirations and self-judgments of a soul marvellously simple and intensely human, gifted with a very genius for human expression. But assuredly these colloquies tell us of true spiritual experiences. Only upon the assumption of pure materialism is it possible to deny communication between man and the world invisible. That people are capable of illusions, none will deny. But once you admit a spiritual world, and that man himself is more than flesh and blood, a being spiritual as well, there can be no ground for rejecting absolutely such spiritual phenomena as are set forth in Fra Giunta's *Legend;* and the question of any particular phenomenon

must be decided on its own merits.   In the
case of Margaret of Cortona, we have a
woman whose public life bears witness to her
practical commonsense : she abhors the
publicity and notoriety which victims of
hysteria invariably seek, and is distressed
when the secret of her life is revealed to her
neighbours ; she is humble and docile, dis-
trusting her own judgment when it seems
opposed to the wisdom of others ; and there
is in her character none of the weak
obstinacy which accompanies nerve-disorder.
In her mental outlook there is the perennial
buoyancy and freshness of a mind strong
and alert.   By all signs, therefore, Margaret
was a woman of strong mind and healthy
emotion, and her colloquies genuine experiences.

To those, then, who seek in the following
legend a further knowledge of the ways of
God with man I offer this book ; and
especially to one who taught me to revere
the great Tuscan penitent, and to see in
her story another page of that most marvellous chapter of evangelical history—the
story of St. Francis and his Order.   For, in
truth, Margaret gives to the Franciscan legend
a certain completion of human and Divine
experience, even as Magdalene may be said

to complete the history of our Lord's mission in Galilee. And just as the Franciscan legend is but a reproduction on another and nearer historical canvas of the picture of the Galilean ministry, so is Margaret but a reproduction, in a more manifest revelation, of the Galilean Magdalene. In Christ's dealings with Margaret we learn His dealings with her who knelt at His feet in the house of the Pharisee, and with all who, like her, kneel at His feet in penitent love.

St. Margaret's legend is something more even than the story of a particular soul—it is a revelation of God's ways with men.

Wherefore, reader, before you pass into the inner sanctuary of Margaret's life, I bid you approach with all reverence, as befits the unveiling of a soul's mystery.

St. Margaret of Cortona : Her Legend, Adapted and Translated.

I.

In 1277, Margaret, being now wholly dedicated to God, and having taken the habit of the Third Order of St. Francis, prays before the crucifix in the Church of the Friars Minor.—Leg. i. 1.

In the year 1277, Margaret, now wholly dedicated to the Christ God, pure in mind and fervent of heart, was praying before the crucifix which is now on the side altar of the Church of the Friars Minor, when she seemed to hear these words : "What is thy wish, *poverella ?*" And the Saint, enlightened by the Holy Spirit, replied : "I neither seek nor wish for aught but only Thee, my Lord Jesus."

She had but a short while before taken the habit of the Third Order of our Father the Blessed Francis.   With pleading prayers she then knelt before Fra Rainaldo, of happy memory, the Custos of Arezzo,* and, with clasped hands and with tears, dedicated herself body and soul to the said Order.

* The various provinces of the Franciscan Order were formerly divided into " custodies," over each of which was placed a Superior called the "Custos," who, in subordination to the Minister-Provincial, had a sort of appellate jurisdiction over the houses of his custody. Thus, the Franciscan Province of England before the Reformation was divided into eight "custodies."   The custody of Arezzo was in the Province of Tuscany.

II.

*Our Lord recalls to Margaret's memory all the
graces of her vocation. Her return in desolation to
her father at Laviano. His unfatherly reception.
Her desolation in the garden, and temptation.
Inspiration to put herself under the Friars Minor
at Cortona. Her obedience to grace. Her filial
reverence, contrition, and abasement. Her detachment from the world. Her deliverance from danger
at night on the water. Interior graces, while still
in the darkness of sin. Her deep humility and
extreme penance. Her pleading to receive the
habit of the Sisters of Penance.*—Leg. i. 2.

Now, one day after this Margaret was in
prayer, when the Lord recalled to her
grateful memory the history of her vocation,
in which, as is quite clear, He included even
the years before her conversion; for He
spoke in this order :

Remember, *poverella,* the manifold ways of
grace by which light was given to thy soul,
that thou mightest be led back to Me. For,
thy tempter being dead, thou didst return to
thy father at Laviano, with thy whole being
filled with sorrow, with thy tears and drawn

face, clothed in a black robe, and utterly ashamed. And thy father, lacking fatherly pity and urged on by thy stepmother, did drive thee from his house. Not knowing what to do, and being without any adviser or helper, thou didst sit down weeping under a fig-tree in his garden, and there thou didst seek in Me a Guide, a Father, a Spouse, and Lord ; and with a humble heart didst thou confess thine utter misery of soul and body.

Then he, the serpent of old, seeing thee cast out by thy father, sought, to his own shame and thy destruction, to make thy comeliness and youth an inducement to presume upon My mercy ; putting it into thy heart that, since thou wast now cast out, thou mightest excusably go on in sin, and that, wheresoever thou shouldst come or go, thou wouldst not lack lovers amongst the great ones of the world, because of thine exceeding beauty.

But I, who created the beauty of thy soul, and desired again to restore it—I, who loved thee still, by My inspiration enlightened thee and admonished thy conscience that thou shouldst go into Cortona, and put thyself under obedience to My Friars Minor. And thou, gathering up thy soul, didst straightway set forth upon the road to Cortona, and there didst place thyself under the care of the brethren, as I had commanded, and with all solicitude didst submit thyself to their counsel and guidance. Bear in mind, *poverella*, how the beginning of thy soul's recovery was in that filial reverence which I put into thy heart towards the Friars Minor, to whose care I committed thee. In this filial reverence, perfectly cherished by thee, I grappled with thine invisible enemy, and broke the power which thy sad fall had given him over thee. From that time how thou didst tremble and thy face burn with shame when any Friar of the Order of St. Francis came into a church or house in which thou wert, and thou didst even fear to sit in the company of seculars or to speak with them when a Friar was present.

Remember, *poverella*, how then I led thy soul to an utter contempt of all worldly ornaments, and, little by little, did induce thee, in all gentleness and for love of Me, to withdraw from the society of women of the world.

Remember how My grace enabled thy body, hitherto accustomed to delicacies, to abstain, not only from costly meats, but even from ordinary food. And, strengthened by My grace, and made more bold, thou didst even macerate thy body by continued fasts, and didst cast aside soft garments, and thy bed thou didst make of a wattle of twigs or of the bare ground, and sometimes of a hard table, with only a block of wood or a stone for a pillow.

Poverella, remember how abundantly in My mercy I gave unto thee the grace of holy fear, of sorrow and of tears, and how thou didst, with much weeping, question the Friars Minor, thy guardians, whether I, thy Father and Lord, would call thee, an exile in sin, back again to thy Father's house and the arms of My mercy ; and how, in like manner, thou didst question people in the world, and by thy bitter grief move them also to tears.

But fail not to remember, too, how thy sorrow was marvellously turned into joy when thou didst in thy devotion ponder upon the mystery of My virginal birth and the sublimity of My Virgin Mother and the glories of the Saints. These tears were the beginning of thy conversion after the death of him, thy deceiver, who for nine years, against thine own will, constantly laid snares for thy purity and virtue.

Remember, *poverella*, the journey thou didst make alone at night across the water, when the enemy of old would have drowned thee at that very moment when thou didst set forth to renew the sufferings of My Passion. But I, with a Father's pity, did carefully guard thee, and bring thee into safety. And, when thou wert still delighting in the world and wert living in the darkness of sin, I, the Teacher, who cannot deceive, made Myself thy Teacher, and endowed thee with a motherly pity for the poor and afflicted; and I gave thee, too, even then, so great a pleasure in solitary and remote places that, aflame with devotion, thou wouldst cry out: "O, how sweetly one could pray here! How devoutly and grandly in such a place as this one could sing the praises of God! Here indeed might one do penance without disturbance or interruption!"

Remember how, afterwards, whilst thou wert yet in darkness, and living alone in the house of the Ladies Marinaria and Raneria, and again in thine own house, with a ray of My light I did enlighten thee, and thou didst weep over thy fall; and when thou wert saluted by noble persons, or by the common people of the country or town, thou didst expostulate with them, saying that, if they knew what a guilty life thou hadst led, they ought not to greet thee nor hold any converse with thee.

Forget not how, when I drew thee away

from thy former state, I placed thee, particularly in the first days, in the company of the noble Ladies Marinaria and Raneria. And remember how thou didst begin to hate and abhor thy beauty, of which hitherto thou hadst such care, and which thou hadst nurtured and sought to increase. But now, by thine abstinence and macerations, thou didst endeavour to destroy it, even going so far as to bruise thy face with stones and to smear it with soot.

Remember, finally, how at length the fire of My love so tranformed thee into Me that, with tears and persistent pleading, thou didst beseech the Father Guardian of the Friars Minor at Cortona to give thee the habit of the Sisters of Penance, that so thou mightest become a neighbour to Me and a stranger to the world.

III

Why the Friars delayed to give her the habit. Margaret's strong confidence in God. Her care to adorn her soul with virtue. Jesting retort before her conversion.—Leg. i. 3.

And now, O reader, why was it that the Friars delayed to give Margaret the habit of penance? Simply because they were doubtful of her constancy and because of her exceeding beauty and her youth.

But the Friars saw how inseparably she was united to Christ, and how she advanced ever more and more in fervour of spirit towards God. And then Margaret would plead with them. "My Fathers," she would say, "you, to whose care I was committed by the Lord, do not doubt me. For even should it happen that for the rest of my life I must wait in great loneliness, yet do I so love my God, and His might has so strengthened me that I fear no creature and no temptation; such is the confidence I have in God, who by His grace has recalled me to Himself. From the time you saw me turn away from the world, I have sought only the company of religious persons, and have changed my life for the better by the grace given me by Christ my Lord. Why then fear? Why delay?"

The Friars thereupon, for the love of Him who had already clothed her with His virtue, hearing these words, gave her the habit. And she, having changed her garments, took care to bedeck her soul with virtue, as will be seen by those who reverently read this book.

Now this change of life she had herself unknowingly foretold. For some women friends, talking with her in the days before her conversion about matters of dress, said to her: "O vain Margaret, what will become of thee?" And she replied: "The time will be when you will say, 'O holy Margaret'; for I shall be a Saint and you will visit me with pilgrim staves in your hands and with wallets hanging at your sides." Which indeed has now come to pass: for not only do men come from many places, but women too in crowds visit her body and the tomb where she lies.*

* Fra Giunta evidently relates this incident with no thought of the spirit of banter in which Margaret made her retort. Many a serious word, however, is spoken in jest, and in all probability the retort bears witness to the spiritual experience Margaret was already undergoing whilst yet her lover was alive, and to which reference is made on page 8.

IV.

Margaret, having received the habit, becomes a new being. The Spirit of Heavenly Love transforms her into Itself. Her intense sorrow for sin when pondering upon Jesus crucified. Her solitude and austerities. Her determination to support herself and her son by her own labour. Her discretion and humility when with others. Her burning words on the mercy of God. She passes her nights in bitter weeping over the blood shed by Jesus Christ. She is seen while in prayer, lifted from the ground.— Leg. i. 4.

When, therefore, she had received the habit of penance, she at once became a new being. For the spirit of heavenly love taking possession of her, so transformed her into Itself, that she forthwith began to seek diligently how she might hide herself away in some solitary place, both that she might shun the converse of those who speak of worldly affairs and that she might enter like Magdalene into more intimate converse with the world's King. Thus, aflame with Divine love, she began to put from her the things which give pleasure to mind or body, that so being crucified to the world, she might come to despise the world. And being desirous of weakening her bodily strength, she fasted without ceasing, macerated her flesh, and chose the bare ground for a couch on which to rest her tired body. Nobody, in truth, is so avaricious for gold as was Margaret for the mortification of her flesh.

That she might the more easily pass the nights in wakefulness, she rarely laid her tired head down even on the stone or block of wood which served for her pillow, though often she was worn out with fasts and tears. But she kept strict watch in prayer from the early hours of the night until the ninth hour of the morning, often weeping bitterly. Many times as she recalled to mind her past sins and pondered upon Jesus crucified, with whom she was now crucified in spirit, she was so broken with sorrow that she feared she would die. Frequently she lost both speech and consciousness, and lay as one dead.

The better to secure herself against interruption and distraction, she chose a small house away from the noisy crowd, but still near to the homes of the noble ladies Marinaria and Raneria, and here she continually offered herself a holocaust to God for love of Him by Whose bruises we are healed ; sometimes scourging herself till her naturally

fair flesh became altogether livid.   She said
that the destruction of her body would in truth
delight her far more than being raised to the
Imperial throne.

But since the beginnings of a conversion
are to be gently fostered (for one attains to
virtue by degrees), and lest the timid should
be frightened from the attempt to subdue
their flesh, I will describe how Margaret
went gradually from one penance to another.

At first when she began her journey along
the road of salvation, the handmaid of Christ
dressed her food with fat on days permitted
by the Church, though she always fasted and
abstained from flesh meat.   After a while,
when she had progressed in the path of
Divine love, she no longer used the fat of
flesh meat, but prepared her food with oil.

Having determined to support herself and
her son by the labour of her hands, she began
in all humility to attend the ladies of Cortona
in childbed.   Yet though for these she had to
prepare delicate foods, according to their
rank, yet she herself always fasted, taking
only lenten food.   But her discretion and
humility appeared in this, that rather than put
the families of the ladies whom she nursed
to the inconvenience of preparing special
food for her on account of her fasts she would

eat sparingly of the ordinary dishes when at table with others, only abstaining from flesh meat.

But when some of the household would come and sing in order to comfort the sick person Margaret would have to retire apart, weeping bitterly ; and the singers, seeing her grief, would themselves be moved to tears, and grieving with her, would stop their singing. For so earnestly did this poor Margaret speak to those about her of the Mercy of God and His austere justice, that nobody could be found, however given over to the delights of the world, who would not lament for their sins as they listened to her burning words.

Every day she diligently gave to Our Lord the full service of the Divine Office, adding thereto other prayers ; yet even so she was in no way found wanting in the service of those she nursed.

Thus, as a lily among thorns, as a light in the midst of darkness, or as gold amidst the dust, was Margaret in the houses where she served; fasting and sorrowing, keeping vigil and working, but never sitting in judgment upon those who ate and drank, made merry and slept. She prepared the scented bath for the lady of the house, but she herself washed in the fount of her own tears, spending her nights in bitter weeping because of the sorrow she bore in her heart at the remembrance of the Blood shed by Jesus Christ : and once a patient saw her in prayer, lifted above the ground.

V.

Margaret leaves service in the houses of others to serve Christ more intimately. Obtaining help from a nobleman, she founds a hospice for the sick in the house of the Lady Diabella. Her love and devotion to the poor. Her own utter poverty. Spiritual favours and consolations granted to her.—Leg. i. 5.

But because of these services in the houses of others, Margaret, the handmaid of God, was unable to serve Christ in the manner she desired or to attend Mass or sermons. She therefore very soon withdrew from the service of the ladies. And, that she might be more free to enjoy the spiritual consolations to which she was now accustomed and also the better to succour those in need, she besought the assistance of a generous nobleman and with his help began a work of mercy in the house of the lady Diabella ; and in this house, the Father of light and pity endowed Margaret with a great love and pity for the poor until the house was turned into a hospice for their use.*

* *Vide supra*, pages 50-53. An account of this work is preserved in a MS. in the Municipal Library of Cortona. (See Père Cherance's *Ste. Marguerite de Cortone*, chap. xi.)

To this hospice Margaret gave her heart. And the hospice was made so utterly the poor's own, that in their hour of need Margaret would have nothing spared, either of the movable goods of the house or of the immovable by which she might come generously to their aid.

Nor was she unmindful of those who had nurtured her in the spiritual life; for she ordered that out of the food of the said hospice the infirmary of the Friars Minor at Cortona should be fully supplied with whatever was necessary for the sick brethren. Truly was she a Mother of Mercy! But, thoughtful as she was for the needs of other poor, she, who was herself almost penniless, would at no time allow any of the goods of the hospice to be assigned to her own use.

In this house of mercy, however, the heavenly Father did not forget Margaret, but gave her a full measure of mercy; for He, Who is everywhere, would at times personally speak with her; at other times He sent His angels to comfort her, and again, standing by her in her struggles, He vanquished the ancient foe.

About the same time Margaret, in all things devoted to Christ, began annually to make a feast for the poor in honour of St. John the

Baptist whom she had chosen as her advocate in heaven, and this feast she provided by the labour of her own hands.

Now in the beginning of her conversion, however weak and sick she might be, she would never take cheese or eggs even outside Lent, nor during Lent would she take even fish. But whenever these foods were sent her she put them aside and quickly seeking out some poor persons gave them what she had, retaining nothing for herself; till at length her charity became so well known that the poor and needy left the doors of the rich and crowded around the door of her cottage in which nevertheless there was but little, and sometimes nothing, to be found. And the neighbouring women, pitying Margaret, sought to drive the beggars away from her door that she might have something left for herself : but she was unwilling they should drive away those whom she loved.

VI.

Margaret, living apart from the world, is not altogether a recluse. After converse with secular people on worldly affairs, Margaret passes a night in tears until contemplating the agony of Christ, when all bitterness of soul passes into the sweetness of love. She goes into the city to beg.—Leg. i. 6.

Though she lived much apart from the ways of men, Margaret was not altogether a recluse. Every morning she went to the Church of the Friars Minor and there she remained in prayer until Tierce when it was not fasting time.* Then returning in silence to her house, she closed the door and gave herself to work and still more to prayer. And as the beginning of wisdom is the fear of Christ and of offending Him, she kept her mind occupied, nor would she gaze upon the face of any one nor speak with any one about worldly affairs. And any day she had against

* That is to say, she remained until the conventual Mass, which ordinarily is said after Tierce, but on fasting days after Sext or None.

her custom conversed with secular people
about matters of the world, the night following
she would in no wise presume to seek from
Christ her accustomed consolations but with
inward grief passed a sleepless night in tears.
And in her sorrow she would sometimes cry
aloud, so that her sleeping neighbours were
awakened. But as bitterness is dissolved
only in sweetness, and the cold passes away
only in the heat, so in her misery would
Margaret pass to the contemplation of the
Cross and Passion of the Redeemer until she
wept most sweet tears ; for in the contemplation of the bitter agony of Christ all bitterness
of soul passes into the sweetness of love.

Thus she sorrowed and grieved, now because
of her sins and again because of the Passion
of Christ. And because she knew that the
mark of love is in one's deeds, and that she
might the better blot out her past life with its
vanity, she went forth into the city to beg,
not entering into any house nor looking upon
the face of any man. Such was her entire
sincerity that she would refuse an unbroken
loaf, fearing lest it should be given to her out
of respect, and she accepted only the broken
bread given to beggars. Afterwards, however,
when she came to hold the poor in greater
motherly love she did not refuse unbroken

bread but accepted it for the sake of the needy.

The more perfectly to fulfil the precept of the Gospel which says : " He that loveth son or daughter more than Me is not worthy of Me ; "* and that she might not prefer flesh and blood to Jesus Christ her Lord, she sent away her only son ;† and taking in his stead the poor, the pilgrim and the outcast, she deprived herself that she might supply their needs.   And at this people took offence and ceased to visit her because she so plainly preferred the love of Christ to the love of her son.   For whilst he lived with her Margaret was unwilling to cook for him lest she should lose time for prayer, and she but rarely conversed with him.   " My son," she would say, " when you come home take what food you find and keep silence, for I will not spend on you the time I owe to the Divine praises." Yet whilst acting thus with her son she did not hesitate to prepare flesh-meat, fish, and other foods for the poor of Christ : for she held that in serving them she was serving Christ, since she did this at the suggestion of the spirit and not of the flesh.   And that she

* Matthew x. 37.

† She put him to school with the Friars Minor at Arezzo. *See Leg.* ii. 7.

might be found ready to enter the heavenly Kingdom, she commanded her son never or very seldom to speak of his father's relatives in her presence, since she wished not to remember them now that she had consecrated her heart to Christ.*

---

* Margaret's attitude towards her son can only be explained by the urgent necessity she felt of curbing her natural affection lest it should again lead her astray. With her great physical vitality and impulsiveness she had need of an extreme restraint which in others might be unnecessary harshness. Later on, as she advanced in spiritual perfection, there is evidence that this restraint was somewhat relaxed in her relations with her son, and she shows herself full of natural solicitude for him. Thus in the *Legend* of Fra Giunta (cap. v. 22) we find her giving thanks to the Blessed Virgin for taking the boy under her protection; again (cap. v. 40) God promises Margaret that her son will become a martyr; in another place (cap. viii. 17) she discourses, with a mother's solicitude, to her son on the religious life; and yet again is this solicitude shown in cap. ix. 28, where Margaret hastens early one morning to comfort and encourage her son who was in an agony of remorse at having half-unconsciously struck his religious Superior.

VII.

Margaret humiliates herself at Laviano. She avenges herself, as a true Christian, on a detractor. Her deep humility when people come to her to be cured of diseases.—Leg. iv. 2.

A little while after her conversion Margaret set off one day for Laviano, her native town, and arriving there, went to the church. And when the Mass began she came with a rope round her neck instead of a collar, and threw herself before all the people at the feet of the lady Manentessa* and besought pardon ; and seeing the greatness of her sorrow, all the people who stood by were moved to admiration and wept with her. Afterwards, Margaret came to love this lady greatly, and persuaded her to take the habit of the Order of Penance, and as long as she lived Margaret gave the lady Manentessa the hospitality of her house, setting before her food of which she deprived herself, and even giving her her own garments.

* Who the lady Manentessa was, and why Margaret went especially to her, I have not been able to discover.

But there was one woman who used to mock at Margaret's humility and love of the poor, and make little of it.   And this was how Margaret avenged herself on her detractor.   She sent the woman her own gown and hood as well as some food she had prepared for her own meal.   Yet this child of the Gospel did not think her revenge complete until, for the greater humbling of herself and to win over her detractor to the charity of Christ, she managed to pay all the woman's debts.   Truly humble was Margaret, nor did she humble herself to evil purpose that she might be the more praised.   For when people, out of devotion, came to her from afar that she might lay her hands on them and cure them of their diseases, she would reply with tears in her eyes : " Nay ; were I indeed to touch you as you desire, or make upon you the sign of the cross, I am certain I should only increase your infirmity, and not take it away ; so great are my sins."

VIII.

Margaret a good listener at religious discourses. While rapt in prayer she is told not to beg any more in the streets of Cortona. Christ assures her of pardon and that she shall be an example of His mercy to sinners. He commits her to the care of the Friars Minor. Her prayer for the Order.—Leg. ii. 5.

Margaret was ever a good listener at religious discourses, which enlighten and instruct the mind. Wherefore, on Sundays and feast-days, when there was to be a sermon in the church of the Friars Minor, nothing could induce her to break her fast till after the sermon, even though it might be in the afternoon, since she was thus able to apply her mind more intently to the discourse and give her whole soul to its enjoyment.

Now one day—it was the day after the feast of St. Thomas the Apostle—she was rapt in earnest prayer when, with her mind, she heard Christ her Spouse speak thus graciously to her : " Margaret, my poor little one, thou must not any more go a-begging through the streets of Cortona, but henceforth thine only journey shall be to the church of My chosen ones, the Friars Minor, to hear Mass and listen to the sermons of those to whose care I have commended thee for thy soul's salvation. And doubt not that thou hast obtained full pardon for thy sins; for already I have put thee as a brilliant light to enlighten those who sit in the darkness of sin; already I have made thee as a furnace to give warmth in the winter of the world, that men may come to love Me and to follow Me with more fervent hearts. I have set thee too as an example to sinners, that in thee they may behold how My mercy awaits the sinner who wills to repent; for as I have been merciful to thee, so will I be merciful to them.

"I commit thee then, *poverella*, as a treasure to My Friars Minor, by them to be instructed and cared for; and I enjoin on them, for love of Me, always to protect and instruct thee in whatever place thou mayest dwell: and their solicitude for thy salvation shall cause their Order to be held in honour throughout the world."

Now, hearing Christ speak thus of the Order, Margaret was made glad; and as a daughter solicitous for her parents, she at once began to commend to the Father in heaven the Order which had given her spiritual fathers on earth.   And the heavenly Father straightway answered her petition, saying :   " I am one with thee in thy prayer, for the Friars whom thou hast commended to Me are My elect whom I love with intimate affection."

IX.

Margaret's prayer to be called "child," instead of "poverella." Our Lord commands her to make a general confession. Her consternation and prayer for light. Her abasement. She receives Holy Communion with a rope round her neck, and hears Our Lord calling her His "child." Margaret's Angel speaks to her and instructs her.— Leg. ii. 6.

But the handmaid of Christ longed to be inseparably united with the Eternal Father as a truly-adopted daughter. She began, therefore, with humble but ardent prayer, to ask that He would, in His infinite love, call her His "child," instead of *poverella*, as heretofore.

As she prayed thus, He, whose love is never quenched, became as a stern judge or as a master correcting an erring pupil; and He said to her: "Not yet canst thou be called a child of Mine, since thou art still a child of sin. But go; make a general confession of thy sins, and be entirely cleansed from all thy vices, and then shalt thou be numbered amongst My children."

At these words Margaret was filled with consternation, and, in a flood of tears, beseechingly besought the Lord, saying: "O Lord Jesus Christ! Thou Who art the True Light, expelling all darkness! Show me, O Thou Who seest all things, and from Whom no secret can lie hid— show me my hidden sins, that I may wash them all away in a full confession, and, in Thy mercy, be made worthy to be called Thy child !"

Scarcely had Margaret uttered these words than the Eternal Holiness, Who was inwardly teaching her, brought before her mind all her past offences which had not been entirely washed away in her former confessions, so that she knew them all, even to the innermost thought. And at this moment the Father of all Mercy manifested to her all her shame, that in the last day the Just Judge might not be compelled to publish her fall to all nations and kingdoms.

For eight days, therefore, she knelt before her confessor, and set forth all her sins, beginning from her earliest years, that so she might become a pure vessel unto sanctification and honour. Then laying aside her veil, she put a rope round her neck, and thus went to receive the Sacrament of the Body of Christ. And when she had received this most living Bread, which gives life to the world, she heard Jesus Christ sweetly call her His child. Such was the sweetness of His Voice that at the sound Margaret was rapt out of herself, and for very joy thought she must die. And in the sweetness of her joy—a joy given to none but those who belong utterly to Christ—she was that day many times raised in ecstasy, becoming unconscious of earthly things, and motionless, as was witnessed by Fra Rainaldo (the Custos), Fra Ubaldo (the Guardian), the lady Gilea, and myself (her confessor).

And when she came back to her external self, she endeavoured to tell us of what she had experienced as far as she could; but words failed her to express what she had heard and said when absorbed in God, and all she could say was : " O the immense, the infinite sweetness of God ! O day promised me by Thee, my Lord ! O word, full of all gladness, by which Thou hast called me Thy child ! "

Having uttered these words, she was again, in the presence of us all, rapt in God—not, as some envious ones related, by simulation, but most truly, as our Friars proved ; for the ladies who were present took hold of her, and shook her, and even pulled her hair. And, when she came to herself, she wonderingly asked her soul how it was that it had not fled her body, hearing the word of Christ the King ? Another time she exclaimed : "O word so long desired, so fervently besought ! O word armed with all sweetness, and joyful to remember ! My child !—and it was Christ my Lord who said it !"

After this, the angel who was set apart to watch over Margaret came to her and spoke many good words, and made her great promises, to the end that she should love Him Who is the Creator and Ruler of all things. And the angel said to her : " I am not thy Lord, but I am the ambassador of the Great King." Yet the joy of Margaret in listening to the angel was but a half-joy compared with what she had experienced when Christ Himself spoke to her ; and she said to the angel : " Thy word does not fill me with gladness as did the word of Him Whom my soul desires." The angel replied : " I am the ambassador sent by thy Creator, and I come to prepare in thee a dwelling for the Eternal King."

Then, taking holy humility as the foundation of all virtue, the angel began to instruct her, and to assist her to cast out all defects and set her soul in order, till, by imperceptible degrees, Margaret became imbued with all virtue.

X.

Now, amongst the mysteries in the life of Our Saviour which Margaret kept continually in her heart, that which she loved most to dwell upon was the wonderful relationship which God so mercifully deigned to establish between Himself and man when He took our human nature ; and she would ponder wistfully upon the condescension of God's Majesty thus manifested to us and upon the dignity of her who in her purity and humility became Mother of God and brought God down to us.

Out of devotion therefore to this mystery she much desired to receive the Bread of Life on Christmas-Day, yet did not dare to approach the Holy Table unless the Divine Shepherd Himself should invite her. And

e better to teach her that this ineffable
icrament is not to be received without due
eparation and a worthy disposition, and
at she might with greater humility come
receive the great King and be the more
ingry for the heavenly food, Christ spoke
us to Margaret : " I reserve for thee this
adness which thou seekest until the festival
My beloved, St. John the Evangelist, but
i that day when thou approachest the altar,
ou shalt experience a new sweetness. And
is My will that thou shouldst not com-
unicate on the day of My birth, because on
at day I would that thou shouldst abide
ith Me in the poverty of the stable where I,
Those coming the angels sang, lay in a
anger between two beasts.

" And thou shalt prepare thyself for the
iming of thy Creator into the dwelling of
y soul in this way : on the festival of My
oto-martyr Stephen,* thou shalt not speak
any secular person, but keep thy soul
itirely recollected in Me. And again on
e day when thou shalt receive Me, thou
ialt observe the same rule inviolably ; that
i I, Whom alone thou seekest with great
esire, may be united with thee by a special
race."

* *i.e.*, Dec. 26th.   St. John's day is the day following this.

So on St. Stephen's day Margaret went to the oratory attached to the church of the Friars Minor to carry out the command of Christ. But she had scarcely entered, when in came the schoolmaster who taught her son at Arezzo, and he began to tell her about him and ask for his school-fees. Now it had been noised abroad by lying tongues that she had abandoned her son and left him in extreme poverty, and that in an excess of sorrow at her neglect the son had cast himself into a well at Arezzo and drowned himself. And this calumny was based upon the fact that the boy had left his school at Arezzo to spend the Christmas festival with his mother, but had not yet returned to his home.

But Margaret, who had cast all her care upon the Lord, and whose peace of soul no worldly anxiety could now disturb, made no answer to the schoolmaster. Whereupon, in the presence of the Friars, he waxed wrath and began to declaim against her, crying aloud that she was proud and ungrateful.

Nevertheless, Margaret, the Beloved of God, remained steadfastly obedient to her one Master, Christ, nor made any reply, not even when the Friars joined their voices to that of the schoolmaster and questioned her. Even I, her confessor, besought her, and so did

Fra Benigno of holy memory. But Margaret did not obey her fathers on earth, because she was at this moment united in spirit with her Father in heaven ; and He had said to her : " Now will it be clear whether thou hast respect for thy son's schoolmaster or for any creature more than for My word." And she had protested that she would in all things obey Him. And so she took no heed of the schoolmaster's declamation, nor of his taunts and threats ; nor even of the Friars when they begged her to speak. At length, the schoolmaster, thoroughly angry, went away ; and Margaret heard the voice of Jesus, from Whom comes all strength and grace, say to her approvingly : " See, Margaret, My child, with what fortitude I have endowed thee and what constancy of soul I have given thee, that thou shouldst find sweetness in silence, whilst bitter tongues were reviling thee ! "

XI.

Margaret prays Our Lord not to allow her again to leave her house, but her prayer is refused. Her ready obedience in spite of bodily weakness is rewarded. Our Lord forbids all unnecessary intercourse with seculars. Margaret's humility and diffidence. The enemy of souls seeks to terrify her. Her perfect obedience.—Leg. ii. 8.

One night, during the octave of the Epiphany, Margaret was alone in her house praying; and she was thinking how necessary it is for those who would give themselves to prayer to live in solitude. Whereupon she prayed to the Lord to allow her never again to leave her house: for, whenever she went to the oratory attached to the church of St. Francis to pray, the women would out of devotion crowd round her, and often she could not pray because of their talk; but in her own house she was far removed from the noise of the world. Moreover, it was with difficulty now that she went to and from the church, for her health was breaking down because of her austerities; and yet again she disliked receiving Divine favours in public.

But the eternal watchfulness of God, which ordains things always at the right moment, and looks rather to the result than to the desire, made her this answer : " Margaret, why dost thou seek incessantly to taste of My delights, and to eschew that which is bitter? Why seek to be shut up in thy house? Go rather to the church of the Friars Minor as thou hast hitherto gone. There shalt thou hear Masses and reverently adore Me, gazing upon Me when I am lifted up by the hands of my priests.* Go forth, and be not a recluse until I will thee to be so."

The following morning, therefore, Margaret went to the church of the Friars Minor, yet could scarcely drag herself thither because of her weakness. But no sooner had she arrived than she was suddenly filled with such heavenly sweetness that she remained there praying until sunset, being lost in the peace which was given her. And in the evening she returned to her house with a new sense of happiness. For whilst she was praying in the oratory her Divine Master, speaking to

* *i.e.*, at the Elevation of the Mass.   Such was the ancient Catholic custom.

her inmost soul, gave her this rule of life: "My child, it is My will that thou shouldst not yet speak with secular people*; and if on account of thy bodily weakness thou needest the help of others, receive their services in silence, or speak to them only in few words and in a low voice. If thou observest this rule, I will reveal in thee great things that shall be of much benefit to thy soul, and not to thy soul only but to the souls of all My faithful. Watch diligently lest thou prefer any creature to Me, and gaze not upon the countenance of anybody, for the less thou hast to do with the world, the more shall I be at home with thee. But by this rule I do not forbid thee to speak with the Friars Minor who are sent to thee, for they are the occasion of thy salvation. Bear in mind how frequently thy converse with secular people has hitherto been injurious to thy soul, and what mischief it has done thee. The more rarely then thou dost speak with them the oftener shall I speak with thee; and then shall I endow thee with most precious gifts." But what these gifts were, Margaret was unwilling to tell even her confessor; partly because it was difficult to name them with human words, partly because of her lowly opinion of

---

* Later on God sent people to her for spiritual instruction.

herself which no favours ever could alter, and which made it hard for her to believe in the promises made her.

Now the ancient foe, seeing Margaret adorned with virtue beyond what is ordinarily given to men, often came to her in her house and sought to terrify her. At one time he would tell her she was deceiving herself; again he would threaten her with bodily injury, and yet again he would predict for her eternal torments. Sometimes he would upbraid her because of her former life and put it to her that she could not possibly persevere in the service of Christ, and at other times he would persuade her to eat delicate foods and be discreet in her penances, until Margaret trembled with fear.

But the Lord, Whose eyes are upon the just and Whose ears incline unto their cry, would come to her assistance. " Fear not, Margaret, My child," He once said to her, " and never doubt that I am with thee in thy trials and temptations." And He went on to show her the gifts He intended to give her hereafter. " Nevertheless," He continued, " if thou wouldst continue in My consolations, avoid conversing with creatures, save only the Friars Minor ; for these are given to thee to increase thy virtue in many ways ; they keep thee true to Me, the Spouse of thy soul, and talk to thee of high and salutary truths concerning thy Eternal God. Yet as I, the Creator, cause all things to live and keep them in life, so would I have thee to love and revere all created things for My sake, and never judge nor despise anyone not even in thy inmost soul, nor let displeasure rankle in thy heart towards anyone."

Henceforth, mindful of the command of the Eternal King, the more Margaret grew in love of God the more compassionate she became towards the weak and the afflicted, and the more she rejoiced in the well-being of her neighbour.

XII.

Our Lord tells Margaret to change her dwelling-place. The objections of the Friars Minor overruled. Margaret's obedience to them commended by Our Lord.—Leg. ii. 9.

Now, Margaret, having been led by the Divine Voice to seek the highest perfection and being placed upon the summit of holy contemplation, one day heard Him, Who is the Brightness of the Eternal Light, saying to her : " My child, hitherto it has been my pleasure that thou shouldst dwell in the house thou art in ; but now I wish thee to remain here no longer, nor will I have thee return to thy former dwelling in the house of thy friends ; but go and seek a dwelling under the Rocca."*

To this change of abode however the Friars would not consent, both because the Rocca was at a far distance from their house, and because they feared lest if she died there her body would not be buried in their church. The Lord therefore said to Margaret : " Let not the Friars be troubled about thy burial ;

* The chief fortress defending Cortona, and situated on a hill on the outskirts of the city.

but let them rest assured that no matter where thou shalt die, thy body shall be given back to them."*

Again the Lord said to her : " Tell the Friars who visit thee that they must have a care of thee for love of Me Who for man's sake came down from heaven, not to receive honour and joy amongst men, but to be scoffed at and to suffer. For I, Whose presence makes the angels glad, came and abode amidst the world's sorrow, and took nought as my share on earth but hard suffering.† But to thee, my child, I have given this grace which is above ordinary graces to dwell apart from worldly conversation and seek solitude ; and thou shalt leave Me to work in thee as I

---

* The Friars' fear was justified, for at Margaret's death her body was buried, not in their church, but in the church of St. Basil near the Rocca. This church, however, was some years afterwards, in A.D. 1392, confided to the care of the Friars. But at the time when Fra Giunta wrote his *Legend*, Margaret's body was still out of the Friars' charge, and this explains his frequent statement that Margaret was committed to the charge of the Friars Minor by God Himself. He argues that as she was committed to the care of the Friars during life, her body ought to belong to them in death.

† This seems to have been a rebuke. The Friars, believing her to be acting by her own will, may have had some thought of relinquishing their charge over her. And it would be only human if they resented the loss of prestige to their church, which her withdrawal would mean. Evidently from what follows the Friars did persuade Margaret by various arguments, especially by an appeal to her gratitude and by reminding her of her duty to other poor souls, not to leave their district, but, if she must leave her present abode, to return to the house of the Ladies Marinaria and Raneria until a further command of Christ should send her to the Rocca.

will, for the welfare of others : because it is I Who lead thee."

Yet another time Christ said to her : "My child, the Friars say they have laboured much in thy behalf ; and it is true. But I, thy Lord, have paid a far greater price for thee, and in far greater labours have stood by and supported thee. And although I gave them to thee as thy guides on earth, yet it is I Who have been and still am the Guide of thy soul. I made Myself thy Leader on thy journey after I had saved thee from the deep into which thy love of the world had led thee. I was the beginning of thy conversion, and the Rule by which thy conversion was perfected ; and I will be both the means of thy salvation and its End. It is I Who have led thee to this house under the Rocca, be-cause here thou will offend Me less and serve Me better. Therefore tell thy confessor and Fra Giovanni * that they put no obstacle in the way of thy remaining here, since thy coming here is My work. And because in in returning to thy first dwelling thou didst act in obedience to the Friars to whose charge I committed thee, My grace shall in no way be taken from thee, nor diminished."

* Fra Giovanni di Castiglione was her spiritual director until his death in A.D. 1289.—Ludovico da Pelago *loc. cit.*

XIII.

Margaret, busying herself with her neighbours' affairs, is deprived of her accustomed sweetness in the service of God. Our Lord tells her that the things of this world prevent her living the life of the Spirit. Further temptations. Comfort from Our Lord.—Leg. ii. 10.

There was a certain time when Margaret was deprived of her accustomed sweetness in the service of God, and she began to be fearful and afraid. In great sorrow she sought out her most gentle Lord, and besought Him to take pity upon her. And He Who has said: "Knock and it shall be opened unto you," answered her thus : " Margaret, thou dost seek Me amongst the things of the earth, busying thy mind too much with the things of this life ; therefore when thou dost find Me, it is amidst the things of the earth. But if thou wouldst seek Me in My heavenly kingdom, keep thy mind fixed on the things of heaven, and thus wilt thou find the spiritual comfort thou art

seeking. For the things of this world prevent thee living the life of the Spirit."

To this Margaret replied: "But, Lord,
am I not separated from the world? and yet
I do not serve Thee."

To whom the Saviour said: "When thou
art hidden from the world, it is true that
interior temptations assail thee, yet it is safer
to struggle with these temptations than to
seek security in intercourse with the world.*
For temptation purifies the soul. But when
thy mind is crowded with earthly affairs, the
dwelling I have prepared for Myself in thy
heart is closed against Me."

After this, the Evil One seeing Margaret
filled with a great peace, moved by envy,
began to assail her with doubts, putting it
into her mind that her whole life was a
deception, and that the sweetness she felt was
not from Jesus Christ. At once Margaret
began to beseech the Lord to guard her
against the wiles of the enemy putting on an
appearance of an angel of light.

Whereupon Christ, as a true lover, com-

* Evidently Margaret had sought to avoid certain temptations
by busying herself in her neighbours' affairs, probably in
external works of charity. In ascetical works this course
is often recommended; but though it is good for beginners in
the spiritual life thus to act, the ultimate purification is only
wrought when the soul grapples with the temptation and
vanquishes it by spiritual means.

forted her, saying: "Thinkest thou, My child, that the deceiver of souls could give thee the good things I give thee, or that anyone can enter into thy soul as I, thy Creator? How could he give thee joy, he who himself is without joy? But he would, if he could, take away thy joy, because he has none in himself. But fear not: I, thy salvation, will not permit thee to be deceived."

XIV.

Christ enlightens Margaret and promises her, as a reward for devout assistance at the Holy Office, heavenly gifts from the Angels and Saints, and that His Angel shall instruct her as to the persons with whom she is to hold intercourse, etc.—Leg. ii. 11.

Now Christ, the Sun of Justice, willed to enlighten Margaret that she might see more clearly ; and one day about the ninth hour of the morning, when she had received the Sacrament of the Lord's Body, a heavenly light entered into her soul and she heard the Voice of Christ saying : "My child, because thou hast so devoutly assisted at the Divine Office in honour of all My Saints, they shall each petition for thee some share in their own distinguishing virtue. The Seraphim shall endow thee with their ardours, the other angels shall each bestow upon thee a gift proper to their own order ; the prophets shall give thee the spirit of prophecy." And continuing He said : "In thy praises keep to thy custom of praising in the first place My Godhead and the mystery of My Incarnation ;

then shalt thou render praise to My Virgin-
Mother, and next after her to thy father the
Blessed Francis.   For it is fitting and pleasing
to Me that thou shouldst put him, thy father,
in thy praises next after her who is thy
mother : for by his prayers he is ever seeking
thy salvation.

" Hitherto thou hast served Me according
to external precepts, and as much by fear as
by love ; but the time draws nigh when thou
shalt serve Me with all thy body and soul
according to the interior light I shall give
thee ; and then My angel shall instruct thee
both concerning those persons with whom
thou must not converse and concerning those
whom thou shouldst honour or instruct.   For
at no time hast thou been so jealous for My
honour as I, thy Spouse, am for thy salvation."

XV.

*Margaret is instructed by her Guardian Angel.
Her deep humility renders her unwilling to receive
the Holy Sacrament. The enemy of souls tempts her
to pride. Her heroic and successful efforts to defeat
his attempts. Her desire still further to humiliate
herself overruled by the Friars Minor.*—Leg. ii. 13.

One night when Margaret was praying in
her own house, her Guardian Angel said to
her : " Know, Beloved of the Lord, that not
yet canst thou scan the depths of the fountain
of divine life nor gaze upon the purity of the
King. Nevertheless take heart and be comforted, for Jesus Christ the Stainless will
bring the hidden things to light and speak
to thee yet more openly and thou shalt
see."

At this time Margaret had arrived at such
a degree of innocence that she could not
conceive how some men are ready for the
sake of any temporal thing to offend God.
" O Father in heaven ! " she would cry, " can

it be that there is a creature living who would willingly offend Thee?" Yet no thought of her own good deeds ever lifted her up, and never did she presume upon her own virtue or merits. She was altogether enamoured of the purity of Christ, and in the love of His purity her own soul became beautiful and drew to her the Divine Lover of souls. And one day He invited her to come and receive Him in the Holy Communion; but Margaret, thinking of the sublimity of His Divine Majesty and her own meanness, was afraid. " Lord!" she exclaimed, " if Thou didst appear in the East and I, standing at the farthest West, should dare to lift up mine eyes to look upon Thy great majesty and purity, surely I should be guilty of presumption." And so there was a struggle in the soul of Margaret; for on the one hand the Divine sweetness drew her powerfully, and, on the other, the thought of her own littleness held her back; for she esteemed herself less than any other creature and yet more guilty.

Now the great enemy, who himself had been cast down by pride, seeing Margaret so humble, thought to tempt her to vainglory by reciting to her the manifold virtues with which Christ had adorned her, and how God had made her so honourable and well-spoken of among all ranks and conditions that great numbers came to visit her. Whereupon Margaret took measures to defend herself. Waiting until night had come and her neighbours had gone to rest, she then mounted upon the balcony of her house and weeping, cried aloud : " Rise up, O people of Cortona ; rise up, I tell ye, and without delay thrust me out with stones from your midst ; for I am she, the sinner, who has sinned before God and man." And then she recited her sins so that all might hear. Her neighbours awakening, listened, and were filled with admiration and compassion for her and much edified. In their own chambers they grieved with her and gave thanks to God Who had placed Margaret in their midst ; but Margaret went back into her house and the proud demon was put to flight.

Another incident I would relate in this place to show to what perfection of humility Margaret had come and how she overcame the pride of the world.

The handmaid of Christ had determined for love of her Lord to remedy, if she could, the evil she had done by acts of an opposite nature. She determined therefore to go to Montepulciano, where in former days she had ridden or walked abroad in all the glory of fine clothes, with her face painted and her hair decked out with ornaments of gold, the gifts of her lover. So now she would go, destitute of glory, with her head shaven and clothed in rags. And as she went, she would beg an alms from those in whose midst she had delighted to act the Lady Bountiful.

She desired, moreover, to take with her a woman who should lead her blindfold with a rope round her neck, and the woman was to cry aloud: " This, my friends, is Margaret who in the day of her pride did so much evil amongst you." After this, the woman should publicly cry aloud Margaret's sins as many as could be remembered. " For," said Margaret to her confessor, "they will then cover me with shame and hard words, and so I shall be conformed to Christ my Lord, Who for my sake bore insults patiently. Moreover, they will think I am gone mad or become foolish, I who before loved to appear amongst them brilliant and witty." However, the Friars, unwilling that a young woman should thus expose herself to the gibes of the crowd, and remembering that an indiscreet fervour often outruns itself, and thinking too that this very contempt of herself might be to her an occasion of vainglory, altogether forbade her doing any such thing, telling her that her good will sufficed, and that to the merit of her good will would now be added the merit of obedience.*

---

* Fra Giunta, we gather from his *Legend*, had more than once thus to moderate his penitent's fervour. Another time, in particular, Margaret was troubled because in spite of her austerities her face still retained its beauty. She desired therefore to wound herself in such a way as to leave scars upon her face. But again her confessor peremptorily forbade her, threatening that if she disobeyed he would have no more to do with her.

XVI.

Margaret's sanctity being much reverenced,
parents beg her to hold their children at the
Baptismal Font. She consents, being unwilling to
pain the Syndic's wife. Her sorrow afterwards.
Our Lord consoles her and bids her not to let her
soul so easily be turned from its purpose. Three
signs of grace given to her.—Leg. ii. 17.

Now because of the reverence in which
they held her, parents would beg of Margaret
to hold their children at the baptismal font;
but she, fearing to be thus honoured, began
to refuse their requests. And this she did
partly because she wished to avoid going
abroad too frequently. But whilst she was
yet pondering within herself upon this matter
and fearing lest in refusing she would leave a
good work undone, she happened to meet the
wife of the Syndic of the Friars Minor,* and
this woman begged Margaret to assist at the
baptism of her son's infant boy. And the
handmaid of the Lord, unwilling to hurt the

* A Syndic is a friend of the Friars, who manages their
temporal affairs.

Syndic's lady, for whom she had great respect, at once consented and went with her to the Pieve*.

After the baptism, Margaret returned home with a troubled soul, and that night she passed without sleep and in tears. Then He, the Comforter of sorrowing hearts, graciously revealed Himself to His trembling child, and bade her in future not thus easily let her soul be turned from its purpose ; and He gave her a command not again to assist at baptisms in the Piève, nor even to leave her house at all, except to visit the church of the Friars Minor, to whose care she was committed ; and there she was to kneel always at a certain spot near the pulpit where she would be hidden from the gaze of the crowd. And He said to her : " My child, three signs of grace have I given thee, which the world may see : in the first place thou hast a greater fear of Me than most people have ; then, thou art utterly ashamed of thy sins ; and thirdly, thou art humble in spite of the esteem in which others regard thee."

---

* La Pieve di S. Maria, the principal church of Cortona.

XVII.

Margaret's abstinence and austerities weaken her so much that her confessor urges her to relax their severity. She replies that she dares have no truce with her body till death. She protests her willingness to suffer and die for Christ. Christ commands her to tell all this to her confessor, and speaks of the necessity of bodily restraint.—Leg. iii. 7.

Now as we have seen, Margaret observed a continuous abstinence, and this, together with other austerities, much weakened her bodily frame.

One day, therefore, her confessor, seeing how weak she had become, sought to induce her to take somewhat more delicate food, but she who had offered herself an entire sacrifice to God, knowing that the enemy seeks in a man's own nature the arms with which to conquer him, replied : " My father, with me there can be no truce in the conflict between soul and body, nor can I at any time afford to spare my body. Therefore I pray, forbid me not to weaken my body by keeping to my accustomed food, for until I die I may not rest from the struggle. Do not believe that my body is so subdued that I can cease exacting from it the debt contracted in the world when it gave itself to worldly pleasure and delights. Be satisfied, I beg of you, that against mine own will, I dress my food with oil during Paschal-tide."

At this she burst into tears and thus addressed her body : "O body mine, why dost thou not help me to serve thy Creator and Redeemer? Why art thou not so strong in His service now, as formerly thou wert in leading me to offend Him? Useless is it to groan and protest that thou art half-dead, for thou must now bear until the end the yoke I put upon thee, as in time past I bore thy yoke to the injury of Him Who made thee."

Afterwards when left to herself she wept inasmuch as she could see nothing good in herself, and in her tears she cried out : "O my Lord King, Glory of the Blessed, O incomparable Jesus, Strength of the Elect! because of the bitter chalice Thou didst drink for me, gladly would I abstain from all bodily food ; nay, gladly would I die to this mortal life a thousand times a day." Then He Who is ever nigh to those who with a truthful soul call upon Him, replied : " My child, thou shalt tell all this to thy confessor ; and this also, that in this life no Christian can be perfect who does not restrain his bodily appetite, for without abstinence from food and drink the war of the flesh will never end; and those suffer most from the rebellion of the flesh who refuse this saving remedy."

XVIII.

Temptations to relax her austerities and be content to be as others who observe the Rule of the Order of Penance.—Leg. iii. 5.

But the deceiver of souls, seeing how rigorously Margaret fasted and how she would in nowise relax her austerity, and thinking not to be vanquished by a frail woman, came tempting her thus : " Miserable woman, what art thou doing in thy house?   Trust, I counsel thee, in the Divine Mercy.   Seek not after great graces which cost so much self-denial and such labour, and are kept only amidst much fear.   Far more prudent would it be to do as others do who observe the rule of the Order of Penance ; fast when they fast and frequent the church for the Office and sermons when they do.   Surely it should be sufficient for thee to be amongst the number of the saved ? "

But the handmaid of Christ, only more firmly resolved to live an austere life, answered thus :   " Tell me, seducer of souls, what reason any creature can have to serve thee, even with the least service? Thou art ever intent upon suggesting evil; but thou canst not create man, neither canst thou redeem him when he falls, nor rule him for his good. Therefore do we listen only to Him Who creates, redeems and watches over us, Who gives joy to those who serve Him, who ennobles and rewards. Whereas they who listen to thy venomous tongue, in this life suffer from the prick of their conscience and afterwards receive the wages of death. Wherefore whilst I live, I will serve only Jesus My Master, with all the powers of my being; for He is my Creator and my Reward beyond measure, and to serve Him is to be honoured upon earth and in heaven. He gave me my rule of abstinence which I will not cast aside; and He has promised me, if I persevere, eternal life."

XIX.

Margaret's sense of her own unworthiness makes her fear she is being deluded by the enemy of souls. Christ proves to her His own presence. Margaret humbly asks how such great gifts can be bestowed on one so weak in body and so unable to do great things for God.—Leg. iv. 3.

Now, Margaret, anxious though she was to gain the heavenly heights, was not puffed up nor did she at all boast of the familiar converse she had with Christ. Indeed, she walked in fear and trembling lest she should be deluded. It happened once, after Christ had been frequently speaking to her about His own glories and the gifts He would bestow upon her, that she, thinking herself all unworthy of a divine revelation, exclaimed : "O enemy of souls, if it is thou who art speaking to me, transforming thyself into an angel of light, I command thee in Christ's name, be silent and depart !" But He Who has regard for the lowly and exalts the humble even to the highest heavens, made her understand that it was He Who was conversing with her, He Who hanging upon the Cross had called her back to life. And He added sweetly : " I, Jesus thy Redeemer, Whom thou dost love and seek above all things, I tell thee thou art My beloved child to whom such gifts have been given as have not been given to any woman now upon the earth."

Whereupon Margaret humbly asked how it was that so great gifts were bestowed upon one so weak in body, who was unable to do great things for God. Jesus replied : " My child Margaret, dost thou not desire Me above all things ? Wouldst thou not willingly die for Me ? Art thou not poor for love of Me ? Is not thy life just one continuous desire for Me, and Me alone ? And dost thou not walk constantly in fear lest in any action thou shouldst at all offend Me ? " And when Margaret replied that it was so, then said the Saviour : " In these ways, daughter, thou dost serve Me and win for thyself My favours. Wherefore love Me as I love thee ; give praise to Me, for I will praise thee and cause all the world to praise thee."

XX.

Christ shows Himself to Margaret as the Divine Babe of Bethlehem. She prays for the people of Cortona. The defects of certain of her friends revealed to her.—Leg. iv. 4.

Once Christ showed Himself to Margaret as the Divine Babe of Bethlehem ; and she, beholding Him thus, was so filled with an excess of sweetness that she was unable to rise up and go forward to meet Him and could only reverently acknowledge His presence ; nor could she speak because of the excess of Divine love which was in her. But as her soul was resting in the delight of His presence, she prayed for the people of Cortona whom she loved (for there was at this time trouble between the townspeople of Cortona and the Bishop of Arezzo)* and the Saviour told her that peace would be established between the people and the Bishop.

Then it was revealed to her that she should not hesitate to admonish certain people, who were her friends, concerning their defects that

* Cortona was in those days in the diocese of Arezzo. It became an Episcopal See in 1326. Vid. Ughelli, *Italia Sacra,* vol. i., p. 625.

they might make a more perfect confession; nor was she to be afraid to manifest to each of them the particular vices which God had made known to her.

But Margaret, accustomed only to judge herself and not others, did not dare to speak to these people, but her confessor urged her to speak, since in keeping silence she was acting against the Will of God and doing her neighbour an injury, and because God would hold her a debtor for the gifts granted her for her neighbour's good. Nor should humility, he urged, be allowed to interfere with the salvation of souls, nor could she without blame withhold remedies from the sick. At last, seeing that she still hesitated, he told her that she might make known to him what the Lord had told her, so that when these people next came to confession he, without mentioning her name, might question them. Thus conjured, she replied : " Father, since you will not mention my name, I will for the good of their souls tell you what has been revealed to me." So when these people came to confess to him the confessor questioned them, and found that what she told him was true.

XXI.

The honours Margaret receives only increase her humility and lowliness. A boy troubled with an evil spirit is cured. Margaret disclaims all share in the miracle.—Leg. iv. 6 and 14.

But now I will relate an incident to show how with Margaret the very honours showered upon her by the people only tended to deepen her humility and self-contempt ; and I take it to be a rare virtue when humility grows amidst honours.

It happened that a boy of Borgo San Sepolcro was troubled by an evil spirit, so that at times three strong men could scarcely hold him. At various times the boy was conjured now by some nuns and again by his relatives to say by which Saint's intercession he might be delivered, and he always unfalteringly replied: " By the prayers and merits of Sister Margaret who lives at Cortona." The boy therefore was carried from Borgo San Sepolcro to Cortona. But when they came nigh to Castel Giraldo, whence one can see the heights of the Rocca di Cortona, the evil spirit, unable it would seem to bear even the atmosphere sanctified by

Margaret's prayers, left the boy, tearing himself away as in a fearful rage and crying aloud: "I give back the boy; take him home again; for I will not be led into Cortona into the presence of that Margaret, whose prayers are as fire to us."

But one of the company out of gratitude to God for the grace bestowed through the merits of Margaret, came and brought the restored boy to her, uttering many thanks; so that Margaret was cast into a great grief and was inconsolable beyond words. Sobbing aloud, she exclaimed : " Do not believe, good men, that the Eternal and Most Wise God, Who never errs in His works, has done this for my sake, who am but a sink of all vices, and an offence in God's sight."

The people, however, not doubting the miracle, went away consoled. Margaret alone remained uncomforted.

Another remarkable instance of Margaret's humble opinion of herself was this: the son of a certain widow fell into the sin of adultery, and what was worse, took away the wife of another man and openly lived with her. But his mother, much grieved, sought by her tears and prayers to soften his hardness of heart, and to get him to send back the woman to her husband and do penance for his sins : but all to no purpose, until one day the son told his weeping mother that he had been thinking of the virtue of Margaret, and he added : " If you can get me some bread from the table of that servant of Christ, so that I may eat even one mouthful of it, I believe that through her merits I shall have grace not only to send back this woman to her husband, but to offer with true contrition worthy fruits of penance to Christ, Whom I have so grievously offended."

Hearing this the mother ran quickly to the house of Margaret, but was unable to get from her any bread signed by her hand with the sign of the cross ; for Margaret refused to sign the bread, saying : " Put nothing near me who am so vile a creature, for whatever I touch is so stained that any virtue it may have had before must at once vanish and be lost." But the mother continued to weep and beg with much importunity till at last she managed to obtain the bread she wanted. And, wonderful to relate, no sooner had the son eaten a morsel of the bread than he was as a new man, strengthened in spirit ; and without delay he restored the woman to her husband, and in all humility hastened to confess his crime.

XXII.

Margaret, after Communion, lays before Our Lord the ideas suggested to her by the enemy of souls and is reassured. She understands St. Paul's " eye hath not seen, nor ear heard," etc. Our Lord continues to fill her soul with consolations, and promises her that, in her own sufferings, she shall learn how great a price He paid for her. She beseeches Him for the Order of St. Francis. He promises a great reward to the Friars who labour for her. Margaret's gratitude.—Leg. iv. 7.

Like Magdalene, however, the more humbly Margaret sat at the feet of Jesus the more did she receive from Him.

One day after communion the handmaid of Christ asked her true Teacher : " My Lord Whom, though unworthy, I have now received ! the deceiver of souls redeemed by Thee hath wickedly told me that if in my accustomed way I seek Thee so fondly I shall become mad." To which Christ replied : " Truly, My child, hast thou called him the deceiver of souls. But have no fear. Thou art My little plant, and I am He who planted thee. Follow Me ; for I am thy Guide, whom thou desirest with a pure heart." Thus

conversing with her Lord, Margaret was all
at once filled with so great a sweetness that
she besought Our Lord not to condescend
thus to her, for that she could not bear it and
live.   And in her ardour she cried aloud :
" Well hast thou spoken, O blessed Paul,
beloved apostle of God, when thou didst say
that ' eye hath not seen nor ear heard nor hath
it entered into the heart of man what God
hath prepared for those who know Him.' "
Then, in the recesses of her mind, she heard
Our Saviour speaking to her, and He said :
" Whatsoever thou hast yet experienced is as
nothing to the joy which is to come."

After this He showed Margaret that
mirror of humility, the Virgin Mother,
saying : " My child, behold I show thee her
whom thou hast chosen."   And Margaret
exclaimed : " Lord, why dost thou promise
such great things to me who am so vile?
and why dost Thou say of this most pure
Mother that I have chosen her as though
this my choice could be precious to her?
Say not, Lord, ' her whom I have chosen,'
but ' the Queen of heaven and earth.' "   To
which the Lord replied : " My child, My
Father loves thee, and so does she, My most
blessed Mother, and so do all the heavenly
court.   But tell Me, dost thou not wish to see

her again ?" Margaret exclaimed : "Lord,
Thou Sweetness beyond compare, I do indeed
desire her, but, perhaps in my ignorance, I ask
not for her as I should ; for it is thus with me,
that when I have Thee Who art the Saint
of Saints, I believe I possess Thy Mother too,
and all Thy court." At this reply Christ
Jesus showed Himself all joyful ; so that
because of the immense spiritual light that
suffused her soul at beholding Him,
Margaret was nigh fainting away. But Our
Lord added : " The day will come when thou
shalt enjoy these consolations without any
hindrance from soul or body." And hearing
this generous promise, Margaret gave thanks
to God in her heart, both for the favours she
had already received and for those to come.

Now when she had thus given thanks,
again the Lord said to her : " Thou art My
child because thou art obedient to Me ; thou
art My spouse because thou lovest Me alone ;
thou art My mother when according to thy
strength thou dost My Father's Will. And I
tell thee there is under heaven no creature
I love more than thee. Yet presume not on
these words, for thou hast still to pay a price
for these consolations—greater than thou hast
hitherto paid. The time is coming when in
thine own sufferings thou wilt learn how

great a price I, thy Redeemer, paid for thee."
Margaret, ever diffident of her own strength,
said : " My Lord, how shall I be able to bear
them ? " The Lord replied : " My child, I,
thy God, have borne greater suffering for thee
than thou thyself shalt bear."

Then Margaret in her filial love for the
Order of her father St. Francis, began to fear
lest sufferings should also come upon the
Order, and besought God on its behalf.*

And whilst she prayed she heard the Lord
saying to her: " I have planted thee, My
child, in the garden of My love ; for nothing
did thy father, St. Francis, strive after so much
as My love. Indeed, so great was his love
for Me that to-day I am loved by none as I
was by him. Know then that the Friars
who labour for thee shall receive a great
reward." Whereupon Margaret replied : " I
give Thee thanks, Most High God, because
of these Friars, inasmuch as for love of Thee
they have laboured much to lead me to Thee
and to keep me faithful to Thee Who art the
Source of all merit."

---

* Probably she at this moment foresaw the calumnies which
would be spoken about her, and which, as we know, did
disturb the Friars greatly.

XXIII.

For a long time this humble soul, destined one day to be so exalted, felt that her soul was like a boat tossed about upon the waters. Hence one day she said to Our Lord: "Abase not Thyself, O Lord, to speak to this vile creature, for I am and ever have been as a darkness under the heavens." But the Lord, hearing her speak thus from her heart, replied: "My child, thou shalt be a light in the world." Then she said: "My Lord, pour down Thy blessing upon all who live in the garden of Thy love, especially those Fathers who have laboured so faithfully for my salvation." And the Lord replied: "My child, I shall bestow upon them special graces for the labours they have undertaken, and I will enlighten them when they preach. And as a sign of this I now bless them on the part of My Father and the Holy Spirit, and on the part also of the Blessed Virgin, My Mother. And because thou hast besought Me that thou mightest be no longer darkness, I tell thee thy prayer is heard ; henceforth thou shalt be no longer darkness but a most resplendent light." Whereupon Margaret asked : "Lord, my Saviour and my King ! With great desire did I offer Thee this my prayer ; and now I beg of Thee, my Lord God, that as Thou hast healed my soul by the sweetness of Thy presence, so now Thou wilt bury Thy handmaid from the world and never permit me to speak of the secret things which Thou dost reveal to me in ecstasy." But the Lord said : "Margaret, it belongs to Me to say whether thou shalt keep silence or speak. Behold, I have given thee My apostles, the Friars Minor, who shall preach abroad what things I have done in thee, even as aforetime the Apostles preached My Gospel unto all nations."

Another time the Lord said to her : " Thou hast told Me I should not abase Myself to speak to thee, but I tell thee that although nothing can be increased or diminished in Myself, nevertheless because of thy life and of My grace which is at work in thee, I shall be exalted ; for many will come to imitate thy life and to honour Me who as yet treat me with contempt and easily offend Me as though I were a weakling or a babe, neither loving nor praising Me, but blaspheming against Me in words and deeds.   But because of thee they will with humble minds and contrite hearts bethink themselves ; and recognizing in Me their Saviour and their God, they will come to love Me fervently, to serve Me assiduously and reverently, and to praise Me unceasingly.   Through thee, many who are now insensible to My favours and too ignorant to desire Me will come to see how sweet it is to serve Me, and with great longing of heart will come seeking Me."

But Margaret only the more protested that she was of all people the most unworthy and the least likely thus to lead others, and she added : "Lord, do Thou make my soul pure, make it lightsome ; for its wickedness is beyond all wickedness, its darkness beyond all darkness."   And again as she was thus praying she heard the Voice of Christ saying to her : "My child, thou shalt be a light to many peoples."

Now Margaret might indeed be a light unto others of virtue, goodness and truth, yet whenever she approached the altar to receive the Body of Christ she was so struck with fear of her unworthiness that she trembled in all her body, and those standing near would be astonished and moved to tears. Nevertheless, the awe in which she stood of that inaccessible Light could not check or diminish her desire for frequent Communion. One day she exclaimed: " My Lord, do I offend Thee by my insatiable hunger for Thee in Holy Communion?" And Our Lord answered: " Nay, but it pleases me much; and for this I bless him who is thy confessor and staff, and I give him a special grace because he has counselled thee to communicate often, and has comforted thee in thy doubt. Fear not: whatsoever I have promised thee shall be done in thee, and whatsoever thou dost rightly ask of Me, whether at thy meditation or at any other time, I shall sweetly listen to and grant."

Now Margaret, hearing this, began at once to beseech the Lord for the people of Cortona, that they might be delivered from the dangers, both within the town and without, which at that time threatened them. Hardly had she uttered her prayer than the Lord, as though wishing to prove the fidelity of His promise, replied : " My child, though on account of their deeds the people of Cortona deserve the evils which threaten them, nevertheless because of their love of thee and the reverence in which they hold thee I shall especially incline to them, and they shall not suffer the evils they fear.   And a like grace I shall grant to all who love and protect thee for My sake. On the other hand, I shall afflict those who by thought, word or deed afflict thee, nor will I hear thy prayers when thou prayest for them."   At this Margaret, who loved her persecutors in the love she bore to Christ, wept, and thus pleaded with her threatening Lord : "O gentle Lord! I offer Thee the prayer which Thy servant Moses offered for his sister when she spoke against him and for all those who injured him ; and I beseech Thee in return for any evil of whatever sort they may do against me and howsoever evil be their intention—I beseech Thee pardon them all, and for the love Thou hast for the Blessed Virgin and all Thy Saints grant them with generous mercy those eternal joys which with tears I daily beg of Thee.   And if Thy justice will not grant them a free pardon, let me suffer the penalty that they may go free."

XXIV.

*Margaret's shame and regret for former pride.
Our Lord comforts her. Margaret, in her joy and
confidence, understands St. Peter's words, and
wishes she could have been on earth to adore Christ
with Magdalene. Our Lord reminds her of His
words to St. Thomas. He claims her greater love
for being planted in the garden of St. Francis, and
speaks of His love for St. Francis and of points of
resemblance in St. Francis's life to His own on
earth. Why men should love his Order. Margaret
is shown the Blessed Francis and a multitude of
Saints, but yearns above all for her Lord. Margaret prays for herself. Her perfect submission to
God's Will. Her humble prayer that none may be
present when she receives consolations.*—Leg. iv. 12.

Another time Margaret, considering how
the Most High God had humbled Himself
for us, was ashamed to think that she could
have in the least ever taken pride in herself,
and having received Holy Communion she
was rapt in ecstasy. And in her ecstasy she
compared herself to dust and ashes, and
prostrated herself upon the ground, declaring
her own worthlessness : "Too late," she
cried, "O Supreme Father of all, too late
have I come to Thee ; too late have I begun
to love Thee—Thee Whom I should have

loved from my birth!"   Then the Lord let her see all the sins and failings of her earlier days, and at the sight thereof Margaret esteemed herself the vilest of creatures and wept.   But the Lord, seeing her struck down with an exceeding fear, gently replied : "Tardily, My child, didst thou begin thy penance, and yet swiftly ; tardily, inasmuch as thou didst delay ; swiftly, because of the ardour of thy love."

At these words, so gently spoken, Margaret rejoiced, and her confidence was renewed, and she called upon the Prince of the Apostles, exclaiming : "Well didst thou say, O blessed Peter, beloved of God! when some turned away from the Fount of Life : 'Lord, to whom shall we go? for Thou hast the words of eternal life.'"*   And she continued : "My Lord, without Whom I could not exist, would that I had lived at that time when Thy Apostle spoke, for I would have adored Thee with all reverence together with Thy most revering disciple Magdalene."   To which our Lord replied : "Hast thou forgotten what I said to My Apostle Thomas : 'Because thou hast seen Me, Thomas, thou hast believed.   Blessed are they who have not seen and yet believed!'   Assuredly, I tell

* St. John vi. 69.

thee, theirs is the greater merit, who now believe though they have not seen, greater than theirs who saw and believed. Therefore, do thou love Me the more, My little plant whom I have planted in the garden of the blessed Francis, and whom I have made to be an instrument of My grace."

Now this loving daughter, hearing the Lord utter the name of her father St. Francis, at once said : "O great and powerful Lord, much didst Thou love my father St. Francis, for with great gifts didst Thou honour him." And the Lord said : "Much in truth did I love him, and much was I loved by him, and I tell thee it is very sweet to Me when men love his Order, because of him whom I have loved in all sweetness. Wherefore be not concerned because thy companion rebuked thee for that thou didst say in an excess of admiration that thy father St. Francis was as a new god : for in some ways I have made him like to Me. For even as I had twelve chosen apostles, so he had and still has many chosen ones ; I gathered around Me seventy-two disciples, but he gathered together so many that the world could hardly count them."*

* This refers not merely to the Friars and Nuns of the Order, but to the tertiaries as well.

Then the Lord showed her the blessed Francis, together with a multitude of Saints, and He asked her why she did not desire their companionship. And Margaret replied : " Lord, I desire the company of the Saints, yea, and of all the heavenly court ; but it is to Thee my soul adheres with constant yearning, for I am made for Thee, my one unfailing and never-ending Good." The Lord replied : " My child, since thou dost seek Me alone I will make thee great in the mansions of My glory, and there thou shalt possess Me in great gladness."

At which word Margaret was filled with joy, not unmingled with fear ; and she said to Christ : " My Lord, Thou hast said truly that I seek nought but Thee. Wherefore I pray Thy Majesty to regard with an eye of loving-kindness my faith towards Thee and judge not harshly my defects." But He Who says not to those who love Him : " Learn of Me to raise the dead to life, to walk dry-shod upon the waters, to cleanse lepers, or give sight to the blind ; " but : " Learn of Me because I am meek and humble of heart," He said only this to Margaret : " Remember, according as My favours increase in thee, so shall thy sufferings increase."

And Margaret, desiring but to do God's pleasure, exclaimed: " My soul is ready, Lord, to bear gladly for Thy Name's sake all pains and torments ; nor will anything seem bitter to me but my fear of offending Thee. But this I ask, O Lord!   Come to mine aid and shield me, lest the world esteem me because of Thy favours ; for in the fulness of my love I speak of them, yet thou knowest, Lord, Thou who knowest all things, that I desire not the praise of the world.   Grant, therefore, that these wonderful consolations which now I receive more abundantly from Thy paradisal glory, may come to me in hidden places, where none may be near to hear me when I speak."*

* This evidently refers to those unconscious exclamations which Margaret uttered when in ecstasy.

XXV.

*Margaret is shown her destined place in heaven.
Her body is raised in ecstasy. Her deep humility.
Our Lord reassures her. Margaret begs to be
allowed to withdraw from the world. Our Lord
tells her others are to be led to Him through the
graces he gives to her. People of all ranks come
from afar to Margaret for advice. Her opinion of
herself becomes more lowly.*—Leg. iv. 13.

After this, He Who exalts the humble
showed Margaret in a vision the place He
had promised her, a place of unutterable loveliness in the choir of the Seraphim. Now of
the beauty of this place Margaret had no
words to speak; she could only exclaim:
" O great Lord! if this place were given to
one of Thy very Apostles, even so the whole
heavens would be astonished; how much
more then if it be given to Me who am nought
but a darkness of sin ? "

In this vision, because of the strength and
gladness of her mind, her body, weak and
emaciated though it was by fasting, now
raised itself erect and stretched out as though
wishing to follow the flight of her soul. And
being unconscious that anyone was standing

by, she cried out : " Now, O Lord, does my soul taste the glory of Thy Paradise and now may it exclaim : 'My heart and my flesh have exulted in the living God!'" Then she heard Christ say to her : "My child, now mayest thou openly tell and proclaim that thou art My chosen one and My true child."

But Margaret, fearful of herself still, even in the heights of heavenly consolation, answered : "My Lord, do not give me so sublime a name, call me not Thy chosen one, me who am the most unworthy of all Thy creatures who are or ever have been in this world."

And here we may remark how Margaret in her estimation of herself was so impressed with her unworthiness that she seemed ever to impute to herself in a supreme degree whatever defects might be found in guilty man. She would speak of herself as though she were the meanest of creatures in respect of birth, manners, and poverty ; and excepting heresy, there was no crime she did not consider herself in some way guilty of. And all this she held as a very truth, nor was it in any sense to her a fiction. Wherefore she would weep and grieve, and it was to her a trouble when she saw that other people did not believe what she said of herself. For which cause the Lord delighted in her, and

on this day He said to her : " My child, thou
sayest that I looked into the abyss of the
world and out of its vileness drew thee forth,
and that I have chosen in thee the vilest of
creatures. But this I have done that I might
make the small things great and the worthless
things precious ; and that sinners might be
made saints."

Yet Margaret, now become as a precious
vessel in Christ, feared all the more because
of her own frailty. Again therefore she
exclaimed : " My Lord Jesus Christ, let me
retire altogether from the world, for I live in
continued doubt of my own constancy. But
if Thou wilt deign to separate me from the
world, I shall no more fear lest I be parted
from Thy Mercy." Then Jesus, the Father
of mercies, comforted His diffident and
fearing child : " My child," He said, "thou
art already confirmed in grace and sanctified
in soul and body because of thy true faith and
fervent desire and of thy pure intention in
every thought, word, and deed ; nor will I
ever permit thee to be separated from Me,
but I will honour thee both in life and after
death." But Margaret only said : " Lord, how
canst Thou bestow such high favours upon
one so vile ? " And the Lord answered :
" Because I have made thee as a net to catch

fish in the ocean of the world : hence My promises to thee are not for thy sake alone, but for the sake of My people who shall be led back to Me. Therefore is it My Will that the favours I have granted thee, and shall yet grant, be noised abroad and published to the world."

Thus the Lord : and who can tell the numbers of those who came to Margaret seeking her saving counsel? Spaniards and people from Apulia, Rome, Perugia and Gubbio, from Citta di Castello and Borgo San Sepolcro, from Florence and Siena ; men and women, clerics and lay-people, even monks and nuns. And yet as soon will you find balsam without perfume, the sun without light, fire without heat, as the heart of Margaret without most lowly humility.

XXVI.

Margaret's diffidence. Our Lord tells her that in Heaven her place will be among the Virgins aflame with Divine love. Margaret's humble remonstrance. She asks if St. Mary Magdalene is among the Virgins. Her unwillingness to speak of inward grace.—Leg. iv. 15.

Now Margaret was in love with most high faith and with humility, but not with her own judgment : hence she never believed in any promise made to her unless it was in conformity with Holy Scripture and the teaching of the Church.

Thus, one festival of the royal virgin, St. Catherine,* Margaret was at the altar receiving Holy Communion when she heard Christ say to her : " My child, thy place shall be amongst the Seraphim, with the virgins aflame with divine love." At these words Margaret was astounded and replied : " Lord, how can this be with one so stained with sin ? " But He Who has promised by the prophet : 'return to Me and I will receive thee,' made answer :

* November 25th.   St. Catherine of Alexandria was held in high reverence in the Middle Ages.   She is frequently found in pictures placed in company with the Blessed Virgin.

" Thy manifold sufferings shall cleanse thy soul from all attraction to sin, and in thy suffering and contrition thou shalt be restored to virginal purity."

Hearing these words, Margaret feared the more : "O Christ, my Master!" she exclaimed, "and is Magdalene amongst the virgins in the glory of heaven?" Christ, the only Truth, replied : " Except Mary the Virgin and Catherine the Martyr there is none amongst the virgins greater than Magdalene." Of this revelation Margaret, because of the lowliness in which she held herself, was unwilling to speak. Indeed she was ever unwilling to manifest the hidden things revealed to her, unless forced to do so by a Divine command or persuaded by her confessor ; or unless she were impelled to speak by fear of delusion, or because she thought that what she heard was not in accordance with the Holy Scripture. And no matter how much her soul might be filled with sweetness because of the revelations made to her, or how clear might be the heavenly light that shone into her soul, nay even though instructed by the Infallible Truth Himself, yet would she not presume to believe anything as true when it seemed to her to be in disaccord with the teaching of Holy Writ.

XXVII.

The greater graces Margaret receives the deeper becomes her humility. Desolate, and in fear, she receives Holy Communion out of obedience to her confessor. Bitterness becomes sweetness, and fear security. She asks if some hidden fault be the cause of Our Lord's silence. Our Lord tells her it was her hesitation in obeying when bidden to receive Communion. He speaks of the purifying power of sorrow. Margaret fears lest she yield to temptation, and is reassured by Our Lord. Fearful of herself, she asks if she has long to live. Our Lord replies : " As long as I will thee to live."—Leg. iv. 16.

But ever as Margaret ascended with Christ into heaven she would descend again into the deep of her own diffidence and humility. Well indeed might she declare with the Psalmist : " Domine non est exaltatum cor meum."—O Lord, my heart is not raised up.*

One Sunday—it was *Laetare* Sunday—Margaret was in great fear and desolation of spirit because that Christ seemed no longer with her : nor would she receive the Holy Communion until forced to do so by her confessor ; and then out of obedience she communicated. And at once all her bitter-

* Ps. cxxx. 1.

ness of spirit was changed into sweetness, and in place of fear she felt security, and her doubting heart became an abode of peace.

But since even then Jesus, the desired of her soul, did not speak to her in His accustomed way, she cried out: "O Jesus, Thou restful Joy of my heart! Jesus, my Peace, my Gladness, my Hope, Whom alone my soul seeks and yearns for! how is this, that though I feel Thee present in my soul, yet my soul hears not Thy Voice? O Thou, Whose Voice softens and refreshes my inmost being! art Thou silent because of some fault of mine which I know not of?" And the Lord said to her: "O disobedient one! why didst thou hesitate to obey thy confessor when he bade thee go to receive Communion?" The humble Margaret replied: "Lord! for this did I not obey, because I thought myself destitute of every virtue since the joy of Thy Presence was taken from me. Yet if in this I have offended Thy loving-kindness, I am sorry." But the Lord said: "Not because of thy reverence and fear was I offended, but because thou didst not obey. And I command thee, My child, as often as thou art told to do anything by thy confessor to obey him; because by a special grace I have enlightened him in thy regard to guide thee in the ordering of thy life."

Margaret, humbling herself afresh before Christ, Who had given Himself to her, asked: "O Creator of heaven and earth, Thou Mirror without speck, my own Eternal Good! how can I, a sinful creature ever battling with temptations, approach to Thine altar and receive Thy Body which Thou didst offer for me to Thy Father on the Cross?"   And the Lord made answer: "Hast thou forgotten that I told thee whenever thou shouldst be in trouble to come to Me, the Haven of Peace?   Have I not told thee thou must needs be purified by many sorrows?   And did I not tell thee too that, though thou shouldst be tried, yet no blow should break thee, for My watchful care keeps guard over thee."

Then Margaret: "Lord, I know mine own frailty, and ever fear when temptation comes upon me that I shall be broken." And the Lord: "O Margaret, My child, well is it for thee frequently to remember thy sinfulness; for the thought of it tells thee what thou mightest be; but My eye keeps careful watch over thee, and My strength supports thee; yet till the day of thy death shalt thou be tried in the furnace of tribulation." And again Margaret asked : " But, Lord, how can so small and fragile a vessel endure the furnace for so long a time ? Have pity upon my weakness and tell me if I have long to live." But the Lord only said : " Thou shalt live as long as I will thee to live."

XXVIII.

Margaret wishes she had never been born because she has offended God.   Christ sternly rebukes her and reminds her that he bestows His gifts where He wills, instancing Magdalene, the Woman of Samaria, the Canaanite, and Matthew the Publican.   Margaret feeling far more unworthy than any of these, Our Lord takes her part against herself.   Our Lord tells her to take His Five Wounds as her weapons. Margaret, contemplating the Wound of His Side, begs for a full understanding of His Goodness and perfect love.   Our Lord instructs her how to obtain both.—Leg. iv. 17, 18, 19.

But Margaret continued to weep for her faults, and one day in sorrow exclaimed: "Would, Lord, that I had never been born, since I have so much offended against Thee and broken Thy commandments." And for this word Christ sternly rebuked her.   Then said Margaret: "O Thou who knowest all things, hast Thou forgotten my wickedness and instability?   Well dost Thou know what I was and still am.   Say not, my Lord, that I spurned Thy mercy and wisdom when I said: Would that I had never been born! for I spoke thus because from Adam until now I can think of no creature less worthy of

Thy gifts." The Lord replied : " Remember that I can bestow My gifts upon whom I will. Hast thou forgotten Magdalene, or the woman of Samaria, or the Canaanite, or Matthew the Publican whom I made an apostle, or the thief to whom I promised paradise ? " " I remember, Lord," answered Margaret, " all these and many others on whom Thou hast bestowed blessings ; yet were they more worthy than I who am so destitute of virtue." Then the Lord, taking her part against herself, said : " My child Margaret, know for a certainty that from the sole of thy foot to the crown of thy head I have clothed thee with grace and adorned thee with virtue." After this Margaret was again thinking of her own littleness, when she exclaimed : " Lord, cast me away from Thee or withdraw Thyself from me, so utterly unworthy am I of Thy presence."*

Now on this occasion Christ rewarded the humility of his Handmaid, for He at once drew near to her and discoursed to her concerning the virtue of purity. Listening to His words, Margaret cried out : " O Lord, Thou alone art the Source of Purity ; Thou alone canst implant this virtue and nourish it

* Compare Newman's *Dream of Gerontius :*
" Take me away and in the lowest deep," etc.

when implanted: without Thee no Saint could ever remain pure." And the Lord replied: " Margaret, if thou wouldst keep this virtue inviolate, take to thyself My Five Wounds to be thy weapons against the enemy." Then Margaret contemplating the wound in His side, said: " Lord, grant me a full understanding of Thy goodness and a perfect love of Thee." The Lord made answer: " If thou wouldst have this understanding and this love, cherish humility of heart, that thou mayest ever attribute to thyself what belongs to thee, and to Me the work which is Mine. If thou wouldst know Me better, begin by loving Me, thy Creator, with a full and fervent heart; then must thou love all creatures intimately, not excepting even the Saracens, whom thou shouldst pity because of the loss of their souls :* for I have created them all and redeemed them with most grievous torments. Wherefore, O Margaret, grieve with all who grieve; rejoice with those who rejoice; and, if thou dost this, I confirm unto thee all the promises I have ever made thee.

---

* The Saracens were at this time the terror of Italy. Vid. Muratori, *Annali d'Italia*, vol. xi.

XXIX.

Christ in Holy Communion bids Margaret rejoice. She humbly expostulates because such mercy is shown to one so unworthy. Our Lord tells her how He bent down to the Saints that they might come to Him. His speckless purity. Margaret's humble reply to a Friar. —Leg. iv. 21.

Now, one feast of St. Barnabas the Apostle, Margaret had reverently received the Body of the Lord, when she heard the Saviour say : " Rejoice, O My soul ! " And she, absorbed in God, thought He spoke of Himself. But again she heard Him say : " Rejoice, O daughter of Jerusalem, because by My grace thou art become to Me as an imperial throne. Worship Me, for I will honour thee ; love Me, for I love thee ; serve Me, for I serve thee and unceasingly minister unto thee." But the handmaid of God answered Him : " My Lord, too great is Thy mercy for such purity as mine ; nor will all Thy creatures convince me that it is otherwise. Nay, willingly would I enter the fire rather than recall my words."* But this she

---

* A reference to the trial by fire, not unknown in the Middle Ages.

said in an excess of humility.   Therefore did
the Lord say to her: " O incredulous one!
how little dost thou know what I have done
in the Saints, and how I have inclined Myself unto them that they might come to
Me; how little dost thou know of My
condescension to many who still live upon
the earth! Wouldst thou have the door of
My mercy closed against thee, that thou dost
speak thus?   But the vision of My im-
mensity and loveliness is thy excuse.   I tell
thee if all the purity of the angels in heaven
and of the Saints, whether in heaven or upon
earth, were brought together, yet would it be
but as darkness before the sun of My
speckless purity did I not incline Myself
unto them.   My child, did I not descend
from heaven to earth and take flesh of the
Virgin Mary?   Yea, O My simple one! and
I thus came down to earth that sinners might
touch Me, and I be a sojourner in their
midst and eat with them.   Say now whether
I have not reasoned with thee and so taken
captive and bound thy heart that thou
wouldst rather enter the fire than hold false
My argument or in any way offend Me ? "

But as a violet in the fulness of its perfume
was Margaret in her humility.   And her
humility differed from that of many other

souls, inasmuch as its greatness was found not so much in outward signs or in words or deeds, but rather in her inmost soul. For Margaret, after the example of Christ, was meek and humble of heart, not by pretence, but truly.

Thus there was a certain Friar who marvelled because after a time she did not speak so fervently of God as she had been wont, and he told her so. To whom Margaret replied simply : " The Lord has acted towards me as does a lender to whom the loan has not been returned ; and who, when he is next approached, will no longer lend. So has Christ deservedly withdrawn from me what He gave, because I am not pleasing to Him."

XXX.

Margaret, meditating upon the sufferings of Jesus on the Cross, learns from Him how and why she too must suffer. She offers willingly to endure torments or even to die. She tells her confessor what Christ had revealed about the Brethren of his Order. She becomes more eager for suffering. Pondering on the insults to which Christ was subjected, she is strengthened by Him. Our Lord explains to her the envy of the enemy of souls. Margaret's reply when tempted to return to more delicate food. —Leg. v. 1, 2.

Now Margaret was meditating one day upon Jesus suffering for us upon the Cross when He, the Conqueror of death, warned her that she too must suffer. "Prepare thyself," He said, "for struggle and suffering, for thou shalt have hardships and troubles as long as thou shalt live. For as gold is cleansed in the furnace, so will I cleanse thee by tribulation and temptation and sickness, by sorrow and fear, by watching and tears, by hunger and thirst, cold and nakedness* ;

* *Vide* Romans viii. 35.

but when thou art cleansed thou shalt pass into eternal joy. But let no fear of these things terrify thee : act bravely and gladly sustain all things, because I am with thee in all thy tribulations. And that thou mayest not faint in thy difficult way, I will oft-times refresh thee by the joy of My Presence." Then said the handmaid of God, straightening herself in the power of her love : "For love of Thee, my Lord, Who hast borne such pain for me, I gladly offer myself to bear all manner of torments, and I am ready with all my heart to die for Thee, O best Beloved !"

These things she related to me, her confessor, but there were many things which happened to her in her sacred colloquies of which she would not speak. But having spoken thus, she turned to me with great spiritual joy and asked : "Dost thou wish, father, to go home to the Friars with a glad heart?" And when I replied that it was so, she said : "Know then from Christ Himself, and do not hesitate to believe, that the Holy Ghost dwells more fully in the brethren of thy Order than in any other body of people under heaven : for such Christ revealed to me."

Henceforth so sweetly did the divine consolations (which are the portion of those who suffer patiently for Christ) fill the soul of

Margaret, that she became even more prompt
to accept suffering for the love of Him Who
comforted her.   And in manifold sufferings
was she purified.   Wherefore one day as she
was pondering on the insults to which Christ
was subjected, she heard His voice saying to
her : " My child, grievous indeed to thee is
the bodily weakness which by My Will is little
by little consuming thee ; grievous too is the
persistence of temptation ; yet grievous above
all and most painful is it when I take from
thee My consolations or delay to comfort thee.
But be not troubled nor astonished because
temptations come to thee ; for the more I fill
thee with delights, so much the more does the
enemy of souls endeavour out of envy to
wound thee with the darts of his temptations.
But thou, My spouse, fear him not, for I,
thine own Beloved, am with thee."

Now, not long after this the tempter came
and sought to induce her to return to more
delicate foods.   And, the more easily to
accomplish his purpose, he suddenly brought
before her imagination all kinds of foods, not
only such as she had seen and tasted, but
even foods which she had only heard of : and
moreover he made her even perceive their
odours.   But the sweetness of Divine love
had so won the heart of Margaret that she

could not for a moment hide from herself the joy she found in Christ, and with tears in her eyes she cried out : " Spare me, my Lord God ; for nothing can refresh me except Thy Presence, in which I find a full and perfect joy."

XXXI.

Margaret draws strength in suffering from the Passion and the sorrow it brought to the Virgin Mother. She prays to be allowed to feel something of Our Lady's sorrow. Our Lord grants her prayer and tells her to go at sunrise, as usual, to the Church of the Friars. She begs her confessor not to leave the Church. Rapt in ecstasy, she follows each step of the Passion. The Cortonese leave all to see Margaret. She herself seems to partake in the sufferings she beholds. At the ninth hour she bows her head sideways, and appears dead. Evening being come, she rises, but seeing the crowded church is in great distress. Our Lord comforts her, and says he has used her as a mirror for sinners that they may learn how plenteous is His Mercy. Margaret's gratitude and willingness. Sudden revival of her bodily powers.—Leg. v. 3, 4.

It was in the consideration of the Passion of the Heavenly King and of the sorrow which it brought His Virgin Mother that Margaret found strength to suffer gladly and without effort. Now, one night in prayer she besought the Lord of His goodness to grant her to feel, as far as she was able, something of the sorrow which pierced the heart of His Mother standing beside the Cross ; nor would she be denied. Then did she hear Christ say to her : " At sunrise thou shalt go as usual to the church of My Friars, and there the scenes of My Passion shall be brought before thee, and thou shalt experience at the sight thereof such anguish and bitterness and pain as thou hast never yet known or felt."

She came therefore to the church at the stated hour and humbly asked for me, her confessor and unworthy staff, and as a special favour begged me on no account to leave the church, as it had been revealed to her that she would that day be crucified in spirit with Christ on the cross.

The Mass was over, and it was near the third hour of the morning, when this devoted soul, becoming absorbed in God, began to drink the vinegar of the Passion. She saw Christ betrayed in the Garden ; then she saw the onrush of the Jews and heard their cries and how they conspired amongst themselves to bring Christ to death. She saw Him saluted by the traitor with a kiss, then led away bound ; and the Jews carried staves and lanterns. Next she saw Him deserted by the Apostles and denied by Peter ; and His Face was bruised. Then she beheld the merciless scourging at the pillar, and saw Christ mocked, blindfolded, and spat upon ;

and they who stood about pulled out His hair and struck His cheeks and in derision bent the knee before Him.   After this she saw how in great haste they set to work to prepare the cross and nails and lance, and to suborn and bring forward false witnesses. But when she heard the words of Pilate : " Behold your King ! " and the reply : " We have no king but Cæsar ; " and again when she heard the words : " I find no cause in Him ; take Him ye and crucify Him "—then she fell into such extreme sorrow and uttered so loud a cry that all who were near thought she was dying.   Then was shown to this soul, transfixed with the sword of sorrow, the Blessed Virgin following her Son bound with fetters ; and with the Blessed Virgin were the holy women, the Marys and the Magdalenes, and they followed in the midst of a crowd of Jews who pressed forward blaspheming.   And from time to time as Margaret beheld this mystery of the Passion, she would exclaim : " Now He is brought forth from the palace ! " " now He is being taken out of the gate ! " " now Simon is forced to help Him ! " " now they are putting the thieves one on each side of my Lord ! " and so forth till the end.*

---

* Fra Giunta includes in his more detailed description how Margaret saw the blind Longinus led forward to the cross

The sight of Margaret thus rapt in the contemplation of the Passion so stirred the inhabitants of Cortona, and so moved them to pity, that many times that day men and women left their work or employment—they even left babes in their cradles and the sick in their beds—to come and see Margaret, so that the oratory* resounded with their sobs. For it seemed to them that Margaret was not beside the cross but upon it, suffering cruel pains.   Indeed such marks of suffering appeared in her that we might well have thought her to be in the very agony of death. She clenched her teeth ; her face became discoloured and her pulse ceased to beat.   She was unable to speak and became quite cold. Even when she returned to herself she could hardly make herself understood, so hoarse was her voice.   At the ninth hour she became insensible and lost her sight, so that she was not aware of the crowd of people around her, nor could she distinguish the voices or faces of the ladies who were attending her.   And since I do not wish to pass over anything which happened that day, I will tell you how

and how she saw him cured of his blindness by the precious Blood of Our Lord.   This curing of Longinus was a mediæval tradition.

* *i.e.*, the oratory attached to the Church of the Friars where Margaret was accustomed to pray.

when the ninth hour* arrived, the hour when
the Saviour, bowing His Head, gave up the
ghost, Margaret also bowed her head sideways till it rested on her bosom ; and the
people seeing her without motion or sensibility
thought her dead.   And so she remained
until evening, shedding no tear.   But when
evening came she rose up as it were from the
dead and lifted up her face now suffused with
the renewed joy of her mind, and gazing
upwards with eyes of gladness towards the
heavens, as one who had received some new
and wonderful gift, she gave thanks to God,
the Giver of all good things.   When, however,
she turned around and saw the crowd of
people a bitter fear took the place of her
great joy, and she began to be troubled in
spirit because of the presence of the people.
But He, the desired Lover, set her fears at
rest, speaking to her and saying : " Be not
afraid, and have no scruple concerning
whatsoever has been done in thee this
day ; for I have made thee to be a mirror
for sinners, even the most obstinate, that
through thee they may learn how freely
My Mercy is opened out to them that they
may be saved."   Hearing these words,

---

* i.e., at three o'clock in the afternoon.

Margaret was grateful to God ; and being solicitous for her neighbour, she replied : " Most High God ! willingly will I remain here or wheresoever Thou dost will, if so I may be made an occasion of glory to Thee or of salvation to the people whom Thou hast redeemed."

Then turning to us who were marvelling at this sudden revival of her bodily powers, she said that she felt stronger now than in the early morning before she had entered into the passion.

XXXII.

When Margaret leaves the Church she seeks, like Magdalene, her Lord of the passers-by. From the Friday to the following Sunday she can neither eat nor sleep. She asks her confessor in the Church if he knew her crucified Lord, and where they had placed him. She returns to her house and shuts herself up. The Lover of souls appears to her. He fills her with joy, and rebukes her because, out of regard to the people, she had lagged behind Magdalene in her quest.—Leg. v. 5, 6, 7.

No sooner, however, had Margaret, who had been in spirit with Christ upon the cross, set forth to return to her house, than she felt the loss of Him and became like another Magdalene drunk with sorrow, and in the excess of her grief she wept and tenderly besought of those she met where she might find her crucified Lord, so that they too were moved to tears. Burning with desire and full of love, she asked of passers-by : " Have ye seen my Lord? Woe is me! Whither shall I go that I may find Him? O that I might see Thee again, my Lord! with what joy Thy presence would fill me! I seek and cry aloud and my heart faints within me ; yet I find Thee not since hard death has taken Thee from me. Where art Thou hidden away? for I would see and hear Thee, yet I hear Thee not and see Thee not!" In this thirst of love she remained from Friday evening until the following Sunday morning; and such was the anxiety of her soul that she could neither eat nor sleep.

On the Sunday morning, when I, her confessor, was preaching in the pulpit of the Church of the Friars, Margaret overcome by fear and shame sought to restrain her grief, yet with difficulty did so. At last, losing herself as it were and abstracted in mind, she asked me in a loud voice if I knew her crucified Lord and where they had placed Him. And as the torrent of her tears fell, those who stood around were much moved and wept with her. But I, wishing no further interruption, told her in a loud voice that the Saviour was so kind and generous that He would not long refuse to show Himself to one who sought Him so ardently.

After Mass she again returned to her house, and again she besought the passers-by to tell her if they had seen her Lord or knew where He was. Then entering into her house she shut herself up with her sorrow, forgoing meat, drink, and sleep.

But on the Monday morning the Lover of faithful souls, Whom last she had seen bruised and in shame, appeared to her in the glory of His risen life, and His Presence quieted the heart of Margaret and drove out all sorrows of mind and body ; and He revealed to her many things and left her filled with a vast joy.   Yet, just as in appearing to the Apostles He rebuked them for their want of faith, so now He rebuked Margaret because out of regard for the people she had not given herself with entire freedom to seeking Him in fervour of spirit, but had hesitated and so had lagged behind Magdalene in her quest.

XXXIII.

The Provincial Chapter is held in Siena. Margaret tells her confessor she knew by revelation that some of the Friars thought the favours she had received were delusions. She says his visits to her will be restricted. This happens as foretold. Margaret's sorrow thereat. Our Lord consoles her by reminding her that He, too, was doubted. Margaret, strengthened in mind, prepares to endure all things.—Leg. v. 9.

Now the Provincial Chapter was being held in Siena when I went one day to visit Margaret in her house. And as she met me she exclaimed with spirit : " My father confessor, I have learned by revelation of the Holy Ghost that the Friars assembled in Chapter have determined to restrict your visits to me, since they have doubts concerning me, alleging what they have read in the Scriptures, and that many people have been known to suffer delusions. Yet the Divine Goodness has so far had regard to me that it will not permit this little plant of yours, commended to you by Christ Himself, to be altogether deserted by the brethren." And

it happened just as Margaret had declared.
For the Chapter being concluded, the Custos
came to Cortona and commanded me on the
part of the Chapter that I should henceforth
visit her only once a week, unless she were
seriously ill or something grave happened to
her.*

Whereupon, seeing that some of the Friars
had begun to doubt Margaret's perseverance,
and to argue that the Divine consolations
given her were possibly delusions or were
frauds purposely devised to win popular
admiration, the devil began to tempt Margaret, and one day said to her that now she
should know that her whole life, with its
supposed Divine consolations, was nothing
in fact but a deception, since the Friars, men of
experience and versed in Scripture and full of

---

* The editor of Fra Giunta's *Legend*—Ludovico da Pelago
—conjectures that the Chapter of Siena here spoken of was
held in A.D. 1288, the same year that Margaret went to live near
the Rocca ; and he suggests that probably Margaret's determination to move to the Rocca, against the wishes of the Friars,
though in obedience to the Divine command, had something to
do with the decision of the Chapter.

In the same year, 1288, on May 1st, Margaret had completed arrangements for the foundation of the Ospedale di S.
Maria della Misericordia.   Vide *Legend*, cap. vii. 26 ; ii. 9. ;
ix. 39.

Three *Custodes* of Arezzo are mentioned in the *Legend* : (i)
Rainaldo da Castiglione, who gave Margaret the habit
(cap. i. 1. ; ii. 6. 9. ; ix. 7.), and died before this Chapter of
Siena ; (ii) Giovanni da Castiglione, probably elected in this
Chapter.   He died in 1289.   (iii) Fr. Filippo (cap. viii. 16. ;
ix. 3.), who revised the *Legend*.

the Holy Ghost, had now begun to doubt her. At this Margaret, overcome with grief and fear, prostrated herself in prayer, saying : " My Lord Jesus, Whom I desire to follow with a pure and simple mind, Whom alone I love, for Whose sake I have not spared my body and have despised all earthly things, Whose Scriptures I have faithfully believed in, so far as in my simplicity I have been able to learn them from the teaching of Thy sons, help me in this new trouble and doubt." But the Lord asked her : " Why dost thou weep ? " And she : " My Lord, Who knowest all things even before they happen, Thou knowest why I weep and that I cannot do otherwise, for that I must struggle against foes who fight against me, and because the Friars to whom Thou didst commend me now terrify me by their doubts concerning me."

Then the Heavenly King Who comforts the weak of heart set Himself before her as a mirror of patience, saying to her : " My child, be not astonished if some of the Friars have doubts concerning thee and argue against thee ; for so it was with Me, the Son of the Living God : some believed in Me and others doubted Me."

At this word Margaret, made more resplendent in suffering, even as the gold in the furnace, became happier and stronger in mind, and from that time prepared herself to endure all things however hard and bitter, confident as one who already is on the road, joyful as one who nears the goal.

XXXIV.

Many coming to see Margaret in prayer are renewed in Divine love. One of Margaret's companions attempts to drive away these watchers. She uses ill-chosen words and thus stirs up indignation. Margaret endeavours to make peace. Failing in this, Margaret sends the woman the supper given to herself, and would have kissed the lips which had defamed her.—Leg. v. 9.

As the days went on Margaret, the handmaid of the Lord, both because of the vehemence of her love for Christ crucified and her sorrow for her sins, added tears to tears ; neither could she restrain or conceal the sorrow of her heart ; and often the neighbouring women, hearing her weeping or speaking to God in prayer, would come with great devotion and, standing at the door, would watch Margaret at her prayers ; and they themselves were renewed in Divine love by what they saw and heard. Once, however, it happened that one of Margaret's companions, thinking to guard her against intrusion, attempted to drive away the watchers from the door, and as she did so she exclaimed against them in words not well chosen.   Whereupon one of the women at the door, waxing indignant, replied hotly and loudly, throwing back words not suited to the place or occasion.

Margaret, praying in her room, wished in her sweet fashion to pour oil on the troubled waters, and told her companion to go and invite the angry woman to pass the night with her.   But a ruffled temper, especially in a woman, sees an insult even in what is well-meant, since it is lacking both in sympathy and sense ; wherefore the angry one began to revile Margaret as a woman possessed by the devil.   But she, the handmaid of Christ, kept her mind securely and tranquilly fixed in God, nor was she moved by the insults, but only the more sweetly sought to soften the reviler, coaxing her to remain and taking all blame upon herself : yet all in vain.   For the woman would neither listen nor enter her house ; neither when the other women besought her would she cease her querulous language.

Margaret, seeing that she could not prevail upon the woman to come in and stay with her, then proposed that she herself should go and pass the night in the other's own home ; but so angry was the woman that she would on no account receive her whom she ought indeed to have invited with humble prayers. But that evening Margaret sent the woman the supper which had been given to herself. In the desire of her heart she would indeed have kissed the lips which had thus publicly defamed her, for she said : " Whatsoever I bear for the love of my Lord Jesus Christ is to me the sweetest of refections."

XXXV.

Margaret's custom of making the Stations of the Cross daily. Her anguish on Good Friday. Our Lord impresses on her that Paradise cannot be realised on earth.—Leg. v. 10.

It was Margaret's custom every day of the week to make the Stations of the Cross;* yet in a special manner did these sacred mysteries renew themselves in her heart on Fridays, on which day, she would say, she could not understand how any Christian could be merry; and on Good Friday she was like a mother who had lost her son.

Now one Good Friday in the depths of her anguish she cut off her hair and ran to the church of the Friars, and she would thus have gone to the other churches but her sense of what was fitting restrained her. Then, as she was weeping over the Passion, the Divine Redeemer spoke to her : " Margaret, if thou wert in a deep, woody solitude on a dark night, surrounded by all manner of

---

* This is, I believe, one of the earliest references to the devotion of the Stations as now practised, though the present form of the devotion is of later origin. See *The Stations of the Cross*, by Fr. Thurston, S.J.

dangers, wouldst thou hesitate to come to Me?" To which Margaret replied at once: "My Lord, I believe I should be like a little child who, hearing its mother's voice, runs to her at once and falls and rises again quickly and runs again."

Then Christ to her: "My child, why dost thou seek to find a paradise here on earth when I denied it to Mine own Body, united though it was to my Divinity? Thou must not hope for this, because on no account can it be granted thee. Thou art like Peter, who having beheld My Glory, on Thabor, wished in the intoxication of his soul to build there three tabernacles, and dwell there because of the sweetness which filled his being. And as his desire was not granted him, so neither canst thou possess here on earth the paradise I have promised thee here-after."

XXXVI.

After desolation of spirit, Margaret finds herself in great peace of soul. Our Lord prepares her for future sufferings and insults. He tells her all shall be made clear in the end, and that she shall leave behind comfort for many. She is not to be curious as to future troubles, but to cast herself into the arms of His Mercy. Margaret suffers insult by reason of her very charity.—Leg. v. 15.

One day Margaret was alone in her house praying, seeking Christ her Spouse, when suddenly she found herself in an entire peace of soul. For she had been in desolation and had cried out : "Come back to me, O most High God! come back to me, Divine Lover of my soul, my Creator and my Redeemer, for without Thee my soul finds no peace." And He, as a spouse hearing the cry of the beloved, at once replied : "My child, I am thy Saviour Who called thee back from the way of death, first when I hung upon the cross and again when I called thee to do penance, even as aforetime I called Matthew and Magdalene. And as these followed Me faithfully after their conversion, so shalt thou follow after Me and be vilified and spoken against by many.   Nevertheless it is not by a martyr's blood that thou shalt go forth from this world as did My Apostle.   And just as they murmured against Magdalene because she cast aside her ornaments and followed Me, so shall men deride thee for following Me.   Yet let not this trouble thee ; for thou art My child, My beloved, My sister, whom I love above all women now upon the earth.* Be brave and take comfort ; for though thy sufferings may increase, so too shall My grace increase in thee, and I will that thou shalt tell thy confessor to signify to Fra Giovanni† that he earnestly pray for thee, inasmuch as thy sufferings will be great and suspicion will surround thee ; even they themselves will sometimes doubt thee, and many will doubt thee until thy death.   But in the end I will

* " Whom I love above all women," etc.—this should be understood as corresponding to Margaret's desire. In the Divine love for souls there is always something special to each soul, corresponding to its particular personality. No soul stands in quite the same relationship to God as any other ; and thus in view of this special relationship, it is true to say that God loves each soul apart from all other souls, and, in a sense, *more* than all other souls. In the case of Margaret, however, the words : "Whom I love above all other women" must be taken in the same sense as the words of the Gospel : "There shall be more joy in heaven upon one sinner doing penance than upon ninety-nine who need not penance." Margaret, set forth in these revelations as a high example of the penitent soul, is undoubtedly favoured beyond other penitents with a manifestation of the compassionate love which saves and purifies.

† Fra Giovanni da Castiglione, the Custos and Margaret's chief director.

make all things clear and thou shalt leave behind thee comfort and blessing for many. For thou art My child, a light set in the midst of darkness ; and I will that thy life be a confirmation of the faith men have in Me, even as the life of thy father St. Francis was in his day set for the confirmation of faith and the support of the Church.   And, My child, it is My will that thou shouldst not be curious to know the troubles which shall come upon thee ; but thou shalt take them as they come, and thou shalt cast thyself together with thy troubles into the arms of My loving Mercy."

Now among those who caused affliction to Margaret was a woman who waited upon her and collected alms for her.   Margaret had told this woman that she must take only a small bottle when she went to quest for wine, and never quest at the same house more than once a month.   But this woman, for her own benefit and that of her children, went frequently to these houses and took with her a bottle by no means small ; moreover, she told lies concerning Margaret.   This the handmaid of God learnt by revelation, and thereupon she humbly and secretly reproved the woman.   But the woman got angry and loudly denied what she had done, and with many cutting words insulted Margaret.   And

thus it happened even as the Lord had foretold, that Margaret would be upbraided by
this woman by reason of her very patience
and charity and humility, and because of her
tears and compassion for others.

XXXVII.

Margaret, after Holy Communion, converses with her Lord and learns how He delights in converse with his friends. She desires to bear extreme pain if pleasing to Him, and begs the gift of pure love. Our Lord tells her five marks of pure love He finds in her. Margaret's fear. Our Lord tells her this fear and her desire for Him take away sin from her soul. She begs for perfect security concerning His promises. Our Lord, while promising strength in suffering, says that perfect security cannot be given. —Leg. v. 16, 17.

One Saturday—it was the Saturday before the twenty-second Sunday after Pentecost— Margaret, having received the Body of the Lord, was filled with an excess of sweetness; and her body being very weak on account of her penances she could not stand. Whereupon He Who disposes all things graciously bade her lay her head upon a pillow, and thus commune with Him in spirit. Then He said to her : " Dost thou believe that I, the eternal and one God, am Father, Son, and Holy Ghost ?" Margaret replied : " Lord, thou knowest all things ; Thou knowest that I most certainly believe. Why

dost thou ask me and cast me into fear?"
"My child," said the Lord, "even so did I
question My apostle Peter, because I delight
in the loving converse of My friends."   Then
Margaret asked: "Lord, how canst Thou
find delight in creatures, since thy delight is
already such that it can neither be diminished
nor increased?"

And the Lord said : "My child, does not
the Scripture say that My delight is to be
with the children of men?   But in thee I act
as I do in order thereby to afflict in thee the
enemy who, being himself shut out from the
joys of Paradise, seeks incessantly to afflict
Me by taking from souls their joy."   Then
Margaret, desiring only to be pleasing to
Christ, replied : "My Lord, though the pains
I suffer should be beyond my powers, yet do
I consider them as nought if they are pleasing
to Thee."   And the Lord made answer :
"My child, much do I delight in pure love."
Hearing this, Margaret exclaimed : "Lord
teach me to love Thee with a pure love, for
this none can have save from Thee, the
Fount of all good things."   "Wouldst thou,'
asked the Lord, "that I make known to thee
the marks of pure love which are in thee?"

Margaret replying that she would, the
Lord thus questioned her : "Art thou not

willing to die for My sake? Is it not sweet to thee to fast continually and to shed tears of sorrow for the honour of My Name? Hast thou not chosen most strict poverty for love of Me Who was poor and needy? Dost thou not shun all worldly conversation that thou mayest more readily commune with Me alone? Is there any pain thou wouldst refuse in thy love of Me?" Margaret replied: "My Lord, because of my love of Thy love, there is nothing, however grievous, hard, or difficult, that does not seem light to me; yet Thou leavest me in such fear that I seem to myself bare of all good."

To this the Lord made answer: "This fear of thine, which mingles bitterness with thy desire of Me, takes away sin from thy soul. Nevertheless, do not doubt at any time that whatsoever I have promised thee shall be done in thee." "But, My Lord," asked Margaret, "how can I be so highly placed in heaven, who beyond all other creatures am so weak through sin? And how can I have confidence who feel no good in my soul?" The Lord said: "Cannot I, the Lord of all, give My treasures as I will? But now tell me whether thou art satisfied with the abundant sweetness of thy converse with Me?" Then Margaret: "My Lord, I confess truly that it is paradise to be in Thy Presence; yet even so I do not believe that one can have sufficient of Thee or that satiety will not produce hunger even in the paradise of the Blessed; for the infinite joy of those who taste Thee draws souls ever more and more to Thee."

Again the Lord asked: "Then thou dost firmly believe and confess that the Father, Son, and Holy Ghost are one God?" "Yea, Lord," was Margaret's reply: "and as I firmly believe that Thou art One in substance and Three in persons, so do Thou grant me perfect security concerning Thy promises." But the Lord said: "My child, this perfect security which thou seekest thou canst not have until I place thee in the glory of My kingdom." Then Margaret: "Lord, didst Thou keep Thy Saints in fear and doubt as Thou keepest me?" And the Lord: "I gave strength to My Saints in their sufferings, but perfect security they had not till they came into My kingdom."

XXXVIII.

Our Lord speaks of those who remain in the fetters of sin, spurning their Creator's love, and of their terrible end. Margaret intercedes for them. Our Lord promises full Mercy to sincere repentance, and says He sends His angels to watch over sinners and urge them to repentance. He gives a message for the Friars. Margaret's thoughts of her own sinfulness. Our Lord tells her He delights in her humility, purity, and charity, etc. He tells her to overcome fears by dwelling on the great things wrought in her, and never to omit her Communion because of her troubles.—Leg. v. 20, 21.

Now the Lord, that He might the better secure Margaret against her diffidence, one day said to her : " My child, why will people bind themselves in the fetters of vice, not heedlessly, but deliberately and knowingly ? Then, after they are bound, they are scourged most pitilessly and drawn from sin to sin ; they are beaten, yet they neither feel it nor resist. To thee, My child, do I complain because of these things and because thereby the people I made unto Mine Own Image are become as beasts. With the wages of hell they procure for themselves glory in this world, but the glory promised them in their heavenly fatherland they spurn as though it were eternal torment.   And yet for their sake I was bound to the pillar and scourged.   But if they of their own will allow themselves to be bound, let them not blame My Goodness.   My child, with reason do I complain : for they call the bitter sweet and the sweet bitter.   Yet to make them free and to lift the veil from their eyes, did I not make Myself a servant and let Myself be blindfold before Pilate and the Jews ? Why then have they spurned their Creator and taken to themselves new masters from those I cast out of Paradise ?   Why have they forgotten Me, their Creator ?   Why is it their bonds are to them so sweet that they will gladly go bound into eternal misery ?   But at that moment when they will hear the words, ' Depart from Me, ye wicked,' they will be horribly disturbed in mind, seeing the Just taken into the Kingdom, whilst they themselves are deprived of their infinite good and cast into the eternal flame ".*

Now, hearing these words, Margaret, as a loving Mother, began to feel pity for sinners, and prayed : "Lord, let not Thy people come

---

* This chapter has reference, evidently, to the people of Cortona.   There is in it an echo of the Good Friday reproaches.

to such a horrible end." And the Lord replied: "The devils by whom they let themselves be bound, scourge them daily even as wheat is beaten on the threshing floor; and they are become as beasts of burden to the devils and bear the burdens put upon them, and yet they will not acknowledge that they suffer. And their lords, having nothing but evil with which to repay them, give them the only wages they can give. For from these masters of theirs come pestilences, and I will not prevent them but let them work their will, till the people and their goods are consumed."

But Margaret, filled with pity and loving-kindness for the people, cried out : "Mercy, mercy, mercy, my Lord God!" But the Lord : "I call them and they will not listen, for they have become deaf to My Voice. Yet I tell thee that however hardened in sin a man may be, if he returns to Me without pretence and with a sincere heart, I will receive him back into the fulness of My Mercy and Grace. Moreover, I send My angels to watch over them and frequently to urge them to do penance."

Margaret, hearing the ministry of the angels thus spoken of, asked : "Do the glorious angels deign to abide with sinners?"

The Lord replied : " Because of the abomi-
nation of sin they do not continuously abide
with the sinner ; but they often come to him
to invite him to return to virtue, and they
endeavour to bring him back to My Mercy.
But at their coming the apostate spirits
tremble and are enraged." And again the
Lord asked : " Why do My children deceive
Me and refuse to walk in the way they
began ? " And he added : " Tell the Friars
that they must preach My Word fervently,
and by their preaching open the ears of the
deaf, and by their example give sight to the
blind."

But Margaret once more turned her
thoughts to her own sinfulness and cried out :
" O Almighty King, great are Thy words ;
but I find in myself no manner of good that
Thou shouldst lament to me because of the
injuries done to Thee by the world. Why
shouldst Thou thus condescend to me ? "
And the Lord replied : " My child, I delight
in thy humility and purity and charity ; and
as for a long time there has been none to
whom such high things have been revealed,
so at this time there is none who suffers as
thou dost. But fear not, for thou knowest
that it is I, thy God, Who watch over
Thee."

At this Margaret exclaimed : " Thou art in truth my Father, my Redeemer, my Light : but I fear lest in my sufferings I in some way offend Thee." The Lord said : " Overcome thy fears and cast them from thee, and think of the good things wrought in thee ; and do not omit thy Communion because of thy troubles."

XXXIX.

Margaret, taken in spirit before the throne of the Mother of God, is sweetly instructed by her. Margaret's thanks for Our Lady's protection. Deprived later of heavenly intercourse, Margaret weeps. An Angel comforts her. Margaret asks what are the signs of an elect soul. The Angel's reply. The Angel names seven distinguishing virtues. — Leg. v. 22, 23.

No sooner had Christ spoken these words than Margaret was taken in spirit before the throne of the Mother of God, and wondering at this sudden change, she asked: "Lord, what means this, that while I was speaking with Thee upon the earth, Thou hast imperceptibly led my soul into heaven?" The Lord answered her: "I have done this that thou mightest the more familiarly commend thyself to My Mother, the Queen of Heaven, and to the Saints who assist at the throne of their King."

Then Margaret turned to the Mother of the Lord, saying: "O Lady of the Heavens, and Advocate of the World! O Mother of my God! thy Son, my Leader, has led me to thee." "And I," responded the heavenly Queen, "receive thee and thy prayers; for thou

art a daughter whom with continuous intercession I commend to the Creator, my Son."

At this reply Margaret greatly rejoiced,
and entered into familiar converse with the
Mother of the Eternal Judge, saying: "My
Lady, my soul has sometimes wondered why
it does not enjoy any converse with thee.
Can it be that in my ardent seeking for thy
Son, I do not hear thy voice?" But the
Mother of Christ replied: "Daughter,
whoever seeks my only Son and Lord, seeks
me; whoever has Him, has me."

Then Margaret gave thanks to the Mother
of God for taking herself and her son under
her high protection.

After this, coming back from the state of
ecstasy, Margaret found herself in her house,
deprived of heavenly intercourse; and she
wept. "Alas! my Lord," she exclaimed in
her loneliness, "where now do I find myself?
Without Thy gracious Presence every place
seems to be an abode of the lost."

But as she was praying an angel came
and stood by her, comforting her. Then
Margaret asked: "O angel of God,
guardian of my soul, tell me by what
signs can the virtuous and elect be known?"
The angel replied: "He is perfectly elect
who has detached his heart from lesser things

and united himself to God alone, so that, by day and by night, his whole soul cries out and sighs for God." Again Margaret asked: What, O Angel of God, are the virtues of the elect?" The Angel answered: "The elect has these virtues: first, profound humility, and this for love of Him Who humbled Himself even to the cross. Secondly, he has perfect charity. Thirdly, in him this word is fulfilled: Blessed are the clean of heart. Fourthly, he denies himself for Christ; dying for Christ, not by the sword or in any such way, but by the mortification of his will; though, should the times demand it, he must be ready to lay down his life for Christ's sake. But he who by penance mortifies his senses, he too dies for Christ. Fifthly, the elect has compassion on the poor, and is not only truthful in his speech but honest in his dealings. Again, the elect, for the love of Christ our Lord, will take to himself all suffering that others may not suffer; he would rather that others should be clothed, and eat and drink, than himself. Lastly, the elect sorrows and is afflicted because of the sorrows and afflictions of his friends, aye, even of his enemies; and he rejoices in the happiness of others and envies no man his prosperity."

XL.

*Our Lord instructs Margaret to separate herself
as far as possible from all but the Friars Minor,
and to suffer with a calm mind such troubles as
come to her. Margaret, doubting how her soul can
be cleansed by her sufferings, Our Lord explains
that they in themselves are powerless, but her love
and His Mercy cleanse. He promises she shall never
offend Him again by grievous sin. Margaret again
begs for entire security, and is told this cannot be.
Margaret begs for leprosy. Her prayer is not
granted.—Leg. v. 29.*

One Saturday before the twentieth Sunday
after Pentecost, when Margaret had received
the Body of Christ, He spoke thus to her:
" My child, separate thyself as far as thou
canst from all intercourse with people except
the Friars Minor. To others thy manifold
afflictions may seem light and of no con-
sequence, but to thee who bearest them they
are indeed heavy and full of pain. And if,
even so, thou dost not suffer all thou wouldst,
yet bear sweetly and with a calm mind for
love of Me such sufferings as come to thee.
But thine interior struggles, wherein thy

soul is being beautified, those struggles, which are more bitter to thee than death, shall be accounted to thee for the martyr's palm."

But Margaret answered: "Lord, I do not believe that my soul can be cleansed or beautified by such sufferings as these." And the Lord: "What thou sayest is so far true, that of themselves these sufferings could not cleanse or beautify thy soul, but thy love, faithful in trial, and My Mercy, these cleanse and beautify. And know that though thou sufferest much because of thy temptations and thine infirmities and thy good works, yet even so I protect thee, and never again wilt thou offend Me by grievous sin."

Whereon Margaret exclaimed: "I give Thee thanks, my most sweet Lord, that Thou dost foretell to me always both the sweet and the bitter things before they happen to me. But I beseech Thee, most loving God, Whom without intermission I bear in my heart by love, that Thou fulfil my desire and grant me secure confidence in Thy protection." But the Lord said: "Thou canst not have entire security till thou art placed in the kingdom of My Glory: and this I will, that thou mayest the better guard the gifts already bestowed upon thee and that so My grace may increase in thee and that thou mayest have a more solicitous care for thy salvation."

Then Margaret prayed that her body might be afflicted with leprosy that so she might not offend Him again ; but this the Lord would not grant.

XLI.

While Margaret is praying for one of the Fathers, Our Lord tells her to warn him to prepare for troubles. Our Lord blesses the Friars because they, above all on earth, imitate Him. He promises a special blessing for their care of Margaret. Margaret longs to leave the world to be with God. Our Lord tells her to remain on earth as long as He wills. She must buy her crown. Margaret once more wishes for entire confidence. Our Lord's reply and promise.—Leg. v. 30, 32.

The night following the Feast of St. Benedict, when Margaret was weeping bitterly because of her compassion for one of her Fathers who was in great trouble, the Lord said to her: "Tell him to prepare his soul, for this is not his last trouble. He shall be tried by troubles within and without, and he shall so taste of My passion that he will fear he must fall. Nevertheless, let him find comfort in Me, for I will strengthen his patience that he may not fall, and in the end he will stand in good stead." And when He had said this the Lord was very gracious to Margaret.

Another day, the Feast of the Finding of the Head of St. John the Baptist, Margaret, having received the Body of the Lord, heard Christ say to her : " Thou hast besought Me to bless My Friars and I, the Redeemer of all, bless them all together by the love of the Elect in whose company they are.   But tell the superiors, My vicars, that they must prepare themselves for troubles, since the Friars Minor, closer than all others upon the earth, imitate Me.   Yet let them be comforted, for I will be with them.   And although I bless others too, yet to them I give a special blessing because for My sake they did not disdain to have a faithful care for thee, My poor sheep whom I brought back to the sheepfold.   Thou tellest Me, poor sheep, that thou wert long in coming ; but I tell thee that one day of reconciliation and grace is more than a year or a hundred years without grace."

Then Margaret, thirsting to be united inseparably to God and to Him alone, cried out : " Lord, when shall I be separated from the world and come to Thee ? "   The Lord replied : " As long as it pleases Me thou shalt remain upon the earth, and, in so far as it is possible to a human body, thou must buy thy crown before thou canst obtain it ; therefore shalt thou still be prepared to suffer." Again Margaret : " So many and inestimable gifts hast Thou promised me, Lord, and yet thou wilt not give me entire confidence." The Lord answered : " I tell thee, this entire confidence which thou seekest thou canst not have whilst thou art in this life." And she : " I ask for it that I may not doubt and be deceived." The Lord : " Thou shalt not be deceived in regard to My promises : this I tell thee."

Again Margaret : " Lord, it is not for myself that I seek this, but rather because of the faith of those who, on account of me, will praise and serve and desire Thee. For, my Lord, whatever I love or desire, I love and desire for Thee and not for myself, unworthy and vile creature that I am." And the Lord replied : " Yes, thou lovest and thou shalt be loved ; thou servest and thou shalt be served ; and as thou dost desire to glorify and obey Me, so too thou shalt be desired, glorified, and obeyed."

XLII.

Now Margaret was ever desirous of hearing the word of God, and this truly is a sign of grace. She was never so weak, never so destitute of energy, but, listening to her confessor speaking of divine things, her soul would be filled at once with joy. And as a garden well-cultivated and rich in soil she would receive the seed of the divine word. She would sometimes say to her confessor: "Fra Giunta, father of my soul, speak to me of God, for the divine word gladdens and inflames my spirit, illumines and comforts it, and at the same time heals my body; for so long as that word sounds in my soul, I feel nothing of my bodily infirmities." Moreover, she carried the name of Jesus ever in her heart, and whenever it came into her speech she was filled with a great tenderness. She would exclaim: "O Name sweet above all names; Name of Him by Whose power I was recalled to grace, by Whose Blood I was redeemed; Whose love of me has drawn me to love only Him!"

Now, one eve of St. Mary Magdalene, Margaret, who before this had been too weak to rise from her bed, was suddenly filled with such fervour of spirit that those about her were amazed; and that evening she passed in great joyfulness, singing the praises of God. Then was her soul rapt out of itself, and she beheld Magdalene the Blessed, most faithful of Christ's apostles, clothed in a robe as it were of silver and crowned with a crown of precious gems and surrounded by the holy angels. And whilst she was in this ecstasy Christ spoke to Margaret, saying: "My Eternal Father said of Me to the Baptist: 'This is My beloved Son'; so do I say to thee of Magdalene: 'This is My beloved daughter.' And since thou art in wonderment at her shining raiment, know that she gained this in her solitude;* and her crown

---

* According to tradition Magdalene, after Our Lord's Resurrection, led the life of a contemplative.

of precious gems is hers because of the temptations she overcame during the time of her penance."

But when the vision passed, Margaret fell back again into her state of weakness, and so weak was she that she could scarcely raise her head.

XLIII.

Margaret prays fervently for souls. Her method of keeping count of her prayers. Her heart is filled with divine love for all mankind, and she continually seeks to benefit her neighbour spiritually and temporally.—Leg. vi. 13, 15.

Now the more she pondered on the benefits which Christ has bestowed upon the race of man, the more fervently did Margaret pray for souls. She was accustomed to keep count in her prayers by a measure of beans which she put into a small vase, taking out a bean at each *pater* in this wise, namely : in reparation for her own sins, which she deplored bitterly, she would say four hundred *paters*; for the Order of St. Francis, one hundred *paters*; for the elect who were in a state of grace, one hundred *paters*; for sinners disrobed of grace, one hundred *paters*; for her confessor, one hundred *paters*; for the delivery of the Holy Land from the Saracens, one hundred *paters*; for those who did homage to the Mother of God, one hundred *paters*; for the children she held at the font and their godfathers, one hundred *paters* ; for the people of Cortona who were kind to her, one hundred *paters* ; and for those who did her injury, one hundred *paters*.

Thus Margaret, having given her heart to God to watch with Him, was unable to repress the fire of divine love which made her open out her heart to all mankind. With all care she continued to study how best to assist her neighbours with the means within her power, now speaking for them in her colloquies with God, now bringing them temporal assistance, and now pouring forth her prayers for them.

XLIV.

Margaret, after receiving Holy Communion, loses all her joy. She is taken in spirit to the Feet of Christ, which, like Magdalene, she washes with her tears. Her longing to see His Face. Our Lord tells her she cannot behold Him as He is. Rapt in ecstasy, Margaret beholds her Lord enthroned, with His Virgin Mother by His side, and is invited to behold the array of the Blessed. Filled with joy, she begs Our Lady's intercession that she may see her Lord. Our Saviour shows Himself to her even whilst telling her to go back into the desert. Margaret's perfect conformity to God's will. Margaret tells her confessor she wishes to retain nothing for herself, and begs that all sent to her should be distributed to Christ's poor.—Leg. vi. 18.

Now on the Sunday after Pentecost Margaret having received Holy Communion with great reverence, her spirit immediately afterwards lost all its joy. Whereupon she exclaimed: "O my soul, let us go to the cross and find thy Spouse, the Son of God." Then, rising from the couch where she was praying and resting, she sprinkled herself with holy water for the washing away of her defects, and going forth from her house she began to call aloud for Christ. That same moment she was taken in spirit to the feet of Christ, which she washed with her tears as did Magdalene of old ; and as she wiped His feet she desired greatly to behold his Face, and prayed to the Lord to grant her this grace.

But He replied : "Thou canst not look upon My Face and see Me as I am till thou art placed in the glory of the Blessed." Then Margaret : "My Lord, for how long a time wilt Thou prolong my Lent?" To whom the Saviour : "Though thy Lent be prolonged now, yet know that thy Easter will surely come." Again Margaret : "Lord, does it please Thee when I speak in the presence of those who are with me of the great favours Thou bestowest upon me?" The Lord replied : "It is my Will that thou shouldst declare these favours when thou art in a state of ecstasy and art unaware of their presence."

Margaret being thus reassured in her mind exclaimed : "Truly art Thou my Father, my Awakener, my Spouse, my Gladness, Joy of all joys!" And the Lord made answer: "And thou art My child, My companion, My chosen one." Then said Margaret : "Lord, send me not back into the desert." The Lord replied : "I send thee back even as a sheep

amongst wolves." Margaret exclaimed:
"My Lord, let this citadel of my body be
quickly destroyed that through the ruins I
may pass to Thee." But the Lord: "And
yet no suffering is so bitter to thee as to
be without Me." Whereupon Margaret:
"Thou art indeed, Lord, my very life,
through Whom I live. If Thou sendest me
back into the desert I shall die. Thou art
my treasure; without Thee all wealth is to
me but direst poverty."

But Christ told her she must indeed go
back into the desert; yet, whilst He said
this, He showed Himself to her, smiling
sweetly upon her. For at that moment
Margaret beheld Him with the eye of her
mind, sitting on a wonderful throne and at
His Right Hand, on a throne of indescribable
beauty, was His Virgin Mother, placed far
above the angels, and she saluted Margaret
and wished her joy. Then the Eternal
King invited Margaret to behold in a
distinct vision the array of the Blessed; at
which invitation Margaret was filled with so
great a joy and her heart swelled with such
gladness that she could scarcely utter the
words which came to her lips: "O my
Lord," she murmured, "Whom alone I love,
for Thou hast created me only for Thee, my

desire is to see Thee Who hast filled me with such joy that I can neither be silent nor speak." And turning to the Mother of God she prayed : " Lady, speak for me, I beseech thee, that thy Son may show me the joy of His Face." And at that same instant Christ heard her prayer and granted her request, and showed Himself to her, even whilst He told her she must go back into the desert.

And at this Margaret protested : " Lord," she exclaimed, " but that will be pain most hard to bear." The Lord said : " My child, remember what I told thee in the beginning when I came to thee, how that thou wouldst be fed on the cross." Then Margaret : " Lord, gladly do I invite myself to this refreshment, and of mine own will I offer myself to suffer all manner of torments for Thy sake, for Thou knowest I seek only Thee, since Thou art my never-failing joy, and without Thee I seem but a lost soul."

When her ecstasy was over and Margaret had returned to herself, she came to her confessor and said: " My father, I wish to retain for myself nothing that is sent to me, whether food or clothing. I desire to go hungry that I may feed the poor, and to go ill-clad that I may clothe them. I wish to exchange for their poor rags any new gown which is sent me that I may abide in want while they have what they need. And I beg my fathers, the sons of St. Francis, that they no more seek to induce people to supply my needs as they have hitherto done, since I would run to Christ, the Desired of my soul, without any encumbrance of worldly goods. And should anything be sent to others that they may supply my needs, I pray you distribute it without delay to my Lord's poor, who are ever in my heart."

XLV.

A Seraph appears to Margaret and fills her with heavenly joy. She beseeches her confessor never to speak of this angel in the presence of other people. She tells her confessor she received from this Seraph a marvellous gift of love.—Leg. vi. 20.

On the night of the festival of the Virgin St. Clare there appeared to Margaret as she was praying an Angel, a Seraph having six wings, who came and remained in her cell. And when he had blessed her, immediately she was filled with so great an ardour of love that for the joy which was in her she laughed. And many times that night did the Angel renew her joy, descending and appearing to her. Afterwards she earnestly besought her confessor never to speak of this Angel in the presence of other people, for that at the mention of his name her heart so beat with gladness that she could not but manifest this joy in her face, however sick she might be at the time. And when her confessor questioned her concerning this new joy, she replied that she had received from the Seraph a marvellous sweet gift of love.

XLVI.

An Angel of the Lord speaks to Margaret, blessing her dwelling and making her great promises. She fears that her Lord will Himself speak no more with her. The Angel reassures her. Margaret fears a joyless Christmas. The Angel teaches her that many who suffer on that day will in the end rejoice. The Angel blesses her. Margaret begs to know the greatness of God's love for her and what is most displeasing to Him in her life. The Angel tells her God will make this known to her in His own good time.—Leg. vi. 22.

Now on the Friday before the vigil of St. Thomas the Apostle, as Margaret was praying, an Angel of the Lord spoke to her, saying : " I bless thy dwelling and all who abide here ; may they be enlightened in grace and cleansed from sin and grow more fervent in divine love." And he promised her great things, of which she was unwilling to speak even to me, her confessor. And it happened in this way : Margaret was calling upon the Lord for that He had withdrawn Himself from her and as yet she had no response to her cry, when the Angel appeared to her sent by her heavenly Spouse ; and he said to her : " I am the ambassador of the Lord Whom thou hast

sought in daily prayer, and I am sent to thee
by thy Father and Redeemer." And the
Angel spoke to her of great mysteries. But
Margaret was afraid because of the greatness
of the revelations and of the promises made
to her; yet did she not fail to give thanks to
God by reason of the Angel He had sent,
and to the Angel by reason of the God who
sent him.

"Praise be to thee, O Angel of God!" she
exclaimed, "for thy abundant blessings and
the words thou hast spoken to me. But thy
words, O Angel, terrify me; for the greatness of the promises thou hast brought me
makes me fear that He Whom alone my soul
desires will Himself no more speak to me, since
He has made so great a promise and revelation through thee and did not come Himself."

The Angel answered: "Margaret, remember what the Lord Himself has told thee,
that until the day of thy death His grace will
increase in thee. And have no fear that thou
wilt be deprived of His divine Voice; but
God will speak with thee henceforth in a
manner above that in which He has spoken
with thee hitherto." And continuing, the
Angel said: "Remember too the words of
the Gospel concerning the love of thy neighbour, which thy confessor has expounded to

thee." Margaret replied : " But who is my neighbour whom I am to love more dearly and intimately ? " " This neighbour," replied the Angel, " is our Lord Jesus Christ, Who for the sake of thee and all mankind was born into the world and was laid in a manger. The light arose amidst the darkness and the darkness knew it not."

Now as Margaret pondered upon the miseries which the Divine Child took upon Himself, she began to fear that for her the day of greatest joy would be a day deprived of joy. Wherefore she told the Angel that she feared this would be to her a bitter Christmas. And the Angel replied : " If thou fearest a bitter Christmas, remember that it did not bring sweetness to Christ our Lord." Then Margaret : " Wherefore then does the Church make so joyous a festival and permit the faithful on this day to eat flesh meat ? And my blessed Father St. Francis said that on this day the whole world ought to make merry since the Light and Joy of the world had arisen."

" Truly," replied the angel, " was the Joy of the world born on this day ; but the friends of God, thinking of the sufferings and miseries into which their King was born, may well be sad. Thou sayest, Margaret, that on this day all degrees of Christians rejoice, but I tell thee much of their rejoicing is not acceptable to Christ the Lord ; for many make festival on this day who in the end will sorrow, and many suffer on this day with the Divine Child who in the end will rejoice.   Wherefore remember the words of thy confessor that thou shouldst have a love and pity for thy poor neighbour, the Lord Jesus Christ, Who on Christmas Day became thy neighbour in the flesh and in the love He bare thee."*

Then the Angel blessed Margaret in the Name of the Father, Son, and Holy Ghost, and in the names of the Blessed Virgin Mother of God and all the Saints.   But Margaret said again : "Call on my Saviour for me, O Angel of God, for He knows my desire and that I dread nothing under heaven so much as offending Him and losing through mine own negligence the marks of His love. And tell me—with all my heart I beg of thee —how great is His love for me and in what my life displeases Him."   Whereto the Angel replied : "God will make this known to thee in His own good time."

* Compare the incident in the *Speculum Perfectionis* (Sabatier), cap. xx., where St. Francis rebukes the Friars for making merry on Christmas Day in worldly fashion.   II. Celano, ii. xxxii., however, gives this incident as relating to Easter Day.

XLVII.

Margaret still desires greater marks of God's love than are given to others. Our Lord teaches her that she has not yet perfect charity. Perfect charity prefers its fellow-creatures to itself. Examples of this. Our Lord forgives this even as He forgave Peter's excess of love, shown by his zeal in the Garden.— Leg. vi. 25.

Much as she wished to see every man and woman in the world holy and pleasing in the sight of God, Margaret yet desired that God should show unto her even greater marks of His love than to others, until one day—it was an eve of St. Clare—she was praying that this might be so and Christ said to her : " My child, thou hast not yet perfect charity, and in thy present state thou must needs walk in reverence even as in charity. And into thy reverence there must enter a knowledge of thyself which will prevent thee from ever asking anything for thyself with forwardness or elation of spirit. Perfect charity is found in the soul which by love is lifted up above itself and so passes unto Me that it prefers its fellow-creatures to itself, like a man invited to the marriage - feast, who allows others to take the most honourable places whilst he himself takes the lowest, or as he who follows the others as they enter the king's palace and does not seek to go before them.   Yet be not disquieted because of this word of thine ;   for even as I forgave Peter when in an excess of love he cut off the ear of a man in the hour of My betrayal, so do I forgive thee now."

XLVIII.

Nevertheless, intent as Margaret was upon preserving the purity of her conscience, she was sometimes rebuked by the Saviour, especially because out of regard for the people about her she would hide or restrain the fervour of her soul in seeking Him. And that she might be the more pure of heart, the Lord commanded her to go to confession not less frequently than once a day ; and He told her to go to her confessor, Fra Giunta, partly because in confessing to him she felt the greater shame and because he, more than her other confessors, did not hesitate to reprove her. For this reason, so Margaret told her companion, Fra Giunta would have a great reward in heaven, and, also, because of his special care of her.

And because it seemed to her that the Divine Majesty was too far above her, and sometimes because of the thought of her own guiltiness, Margaret often abstained from Holy Communion.   But one day the Most High, having pity upon her, said to her: " My child, do not abstain as thou hast done from receiving the Sacrament of My Body; for already thou art so far cleansed from vice that I command thee to receive Me often. And when thou art unable, on account of sickness, to bear the burden of prayer as thou wert wont in the first days of thy conversion, let it suffice by way of preparation that thou confess thy sins and avoid worldly conversation.   Love silence.   And if thou art able to confess thy sins before breaking thy fast, do so;   and hide not thy life from the Friars, thy confessors, that thou mayest not be deceived by any temptation."

Now when, on account of her weakness, she had to receive Holy Communion in her house, Margaret would most reverently prepare herself to receive this most High Sacrament; and before her prayer she would have the whole house thoroughly cleansed from dust.   She said that the ground over which passed the priest who carried the body of Christ should be paved with purest gold.

XLIX.

Our Lord laments the irreverence shown by many when offering the Holy Mass. Margaret's fears of her own unworthiness. Our Lord comforts and blesses her. Margaret marvels at Our Lord's condescension in giving Himself to Judas, etc., and in continuing so to give Himself. Our Lord rewards her for her love and teaches her how to bear tribulation without fear.—Leg. vii., 10, 11.

One day Christ spoke to Margaret, saying : "My child, much do I lament over the irreverence of the multitude of priests who daily hold Me in their hands, yet have no love for Me, and hardly acknowledge My presence.* For, if they thought of it, assuredly would they know that among created things none is more beautiful than the priest saying mass. Yet do many of them not fear to touch Me with stained hands, and to treat Me as less than the dust in the street."

* To understand this chapter and those that follow we must bear in mind the growing worldliness and corruption of the age in which Margaret lived. It was an age of great saints and great sinners; of strong faith in some, of increasing indifference among the many.

Hearing these words, Margaret was struck with a great fear, and, thinking of her own unworthiness, she exclaimed: "Why, then, O Lord, dost Thou so frequently invite me, so unworthy, nay, even constrain me, to receive Thy Sacred Body?" The Lord replied: "My child, I, the Eternal Son of God, born into the world of a Virgin, have cleansed thee from thy sins. And now I bless thee on the part of My Father, on My own part, and on that of the Holy Ghost; and in the name too of My most blessed Mother."

Another day after receiving Holy Communion, Margaret was wondering at the sublime condescension of the Son of God, when she exclaimed : "Why, O Lord, didst Thou humble Thyself so greatly at Thy Last Supper to Judas and the others ; and why dost Thou continue even now to give Thyself to us?" And the Lord made answer: "My child, truly are there to-day many Judases to whom it is permitted to receive Me and touch Me. But thou out of thy love for Me hast stripped thyself often and made thyself a beggar ; therefore will I clothe thee with grace and enrich thy soul. And now, fear not whatever tribulation may come upon thee, for in thy tribulations thou art made acceptable to Me, and united to Me in love."

Then, having received her accustomed blessing, she heard Christ speaking and promising her great things ; but in her humility she would not speak of these things, even to her confessor.

L.

Our Lord asks Margaret if she truly believes that He is the Lord her God. He speaks of the many to whom He is dead and the few in whom He lives by grace. Of unworthy communicants. Our Lord gives Margaret a message to her confessor about those to whom he is not to give Holy Communion. The Communions of worldlings and their lives. Divine favours to be granted less frequently to Margaret for two reasons. A message to Fra Giunta.—Leg. viii. 15.

Now on the eighteenth Sunday after Pentecost, Margaret heard the voice of the Saviour asking her : " My child, dost thou truly believe that I am the Lord thy God ? " Margaret replied : " My Creator, my Father, true Joy of my heart, why dost Thou ask me such a question ? " And the Lord : " Because, My child, with most men I am dead as far as they can make me so, and few are they in whom I live by grace. So greatly do they offend Me that were I, the true God, to forget that I came to suffer for them, surely would I hiss them away from My Presence when they come to communicate ; such is the horror of their sins. For in receiving Me unworthily they again crucify Me and give Me to drink of a more bitter cup than that which the Jews offered Me. But as I permitted the Jews to take hold of Me and drag Me through the city to Calvary, so now do I suffer injury from those who receive me without devotion, and who handle Me irreverently. Hence thou shalt tell thy confessor that I command him never again to give the Communion of My Body to any person, whether religious or secular, unless she first cease to paint or adorn her face, or at least be prepared to do so ; and unless, moreover, he be disposed to obey My commandments and to do My Will. For the Communions of worldlings and their lives are an exceeding offence to Me. Woe to souls who cease not to offend Me and yet presume to receive My Body, for it will go hard with them at their judgment. And as to the knowledge of souls which is given thee, know that this is a high degree of perfection, as Fra Giunta has told thee. Yet prepare thyself for suffering ; for many people shall come to regard thee with contempt. But their evil-speaking of thee shall be to thee in place of the martyrdom which many suffered for Me in ancient days. And again, because of thy fear of offending

Me, even slight hardships will appear to thee great. But fear not, My child, My companion, My sister, if in the sight of the world My favours are less frequently granted thee. For this shall be that the world may despise thee and thou be made more secure in My grace. And tell Fra Giunta to prepare himself diligently when he says Mass, and to take comfort in adversity by recalling to mind how I suffered ; and let him have a diligent care to conquer himself."

LI.

Margaret fears to receive Holy Communion, Our Lord having taken His consolations from her. Her confessor gives her confidence. She then goes to confession, and is told to at once receive Holy Communion. Not finding her accustomed consolation, she weeps full of fear. Our Saviour admonishes and instructs her. He tells her she shall be a ladder by which sinners shall mount to Him. Our Lord tells her she ought to pray for her confessor, being so much beholden to him.—Leg. vii. 20.

One feast of the Purification of the spotless Mother of God, I, her confessor, found Margaret hungry for the Communion of the Body of Christ; yet did she fear to receive, thinking in her humility that she must be displeasing to God since he had taken from her His consolations. Then I talked with her about the Holy Scriptures, until she had gained great confidence and asked to go to confession. And when I had given her absolution, I commanded her to go at once and receive the Holy Communion, even though she might not feel the consolations she had been accustomed to feel in the early days of her conversion.   For in the Holy Communion, I told her, she would receive new grace and be strengthened against the temptations of the evil one.   Whereupon she went to the priest and received from his hand the Body of the Lord.   But when she found not her accustomed consolation she was full of fear and wept.

Then Christ spoke to her : " My child," He said, " be not astonished that thou didst not feel more quickly the joy of My Presence ; for when thou didst come to receive Me thy soul was not fully prepared, and I give Myself to thee in such wise as thou art prepared to receive Me."   Margaret made answer : " Lord, I was afraid to receive Thee because it seemed to me my soul was not prepared for so high a Guest."   And the Lord : " My child, it pleases Me that thou shouldst receive Me, and in giving Myself to thee and drawing thee to Me, I give myself to the mother of sinners.   For I have made thee to be as a mother to those who have sinned ; and in keeping thee away from Me it is as though the evil one had kept Me from Mine own mother."

At these words, Margaret was struck with unspeakable astonishment ; but Christ continued : " As the most blessed Virgin was chosen to be My Mother according to the flesh for the sake of all mankind, so art thou chosen to be in thine own fashion a mirror for sinners and their mother.   For by My grace thou art become most beautiful before Me in heaven, and I will make thee holy upon the earth.   Nay, I will not say I will make thee holy, for already by My mercy thou art holy.   To thyself thou seemest poor in that it seems to thee that thou dost not yet possess Me ; nevertheless, I have enriched thee beyond words.   My child, in whom my Spirit finds rest, I will not call thee a lily of the garden but a lily of the broad fields, for thy perfume will be carried far, and many who now feel not My presence will, through thee, come to know Me.   And the perfume of thy name shall be carried amongst all peoples, even as the breeze carries the perfume of the lily far and wide."

Now as Margaret wondered to herself why it was that at times she felt the sweetness of Christ's Presence and at other times felt it not, Christ Himself answered her : " Thou findest Me such as I find thee.   In these days thy mind is distracted, weary with many labours.   Behold Magdalene : to her did I show Myself in the Garden after my Resurrection in such way as I was already in her soul. But now I have put thee in the world to be a ladder by which sinners shall mount to Me." Margaret replied : " Lord, what can sinners behold in me for their example ? " The Lord made answer : " They will imitate thine abstinences and fasts, thy humility and patience in suffering, thy gentleness of speech, and thy meekness. They will imitate too thy sincerity and the solicitude with which thou dost shun the world."

Now Margaret during this colloquy did not, as was her wont, beseech the Lord for her confessor. Wherefore Jesus, the Ever-Thoughtful, said to her : " My child, thou oughtest to ask a favour for thy counsellor and confessor, for thou art much beholden to him." And she : " Willingly, Lord, do I pray for him, for that I know well how greatly I am beholden to him, and the more especially do I commend him to Thee now since never did he speak to me of Thee as he spoke to-day." " He spoke well of Me," replied the Lord, " because I spoke through him." And Margaret : " Truly, Lord, did I know that Thou wert speaking through him, to my great joy."

LII.

Our Lord tells Margaret she desires too much to dwell apart in the enjoyment of His consolations, forgetting what she owes to His children. Margaret acknowledges her want of charity, and pleads thoughtlessness. Our Lord says those who have charity towards His children have it for Him. He gives a message to the Friars that they are to preach the Epistles and Gospels. They are to preach of His sufferings and death, and, when they preach, suffer in their own souls as He suffered. Necessity of fervour and zeal. Our Lord blesses Margaret.— Leg. vii. 23.

On one occasion when Margaret was in prayer, she heard in spirit a voice saying to her : " Prepare thyself, O star, for the Sun of Justice desires to come down to thee, and to establish in thee His throne, whence He will send forth His rays of justice and loving-kindness." Margaret, ever shrinking from her own praise, replied : " Lord, if it please thee, I will not speak of this to the Friar, my confessor." But the Lord: " Tell thy confessor and the other Friars that they are to hold thee hidden from the world. And do thou hide thyself from the world as far as thou canst.   And yet thou dost desire too much to dwell apart in the enjoyment of My consolations, forgetful of what thou owest to My children.   Well could I have called thee to walk alone in secret and thus have led thee to the kingdom of heaven if I had so willed. But such was not My will."

Then Margaret exclaimed : "Lord, it is the thought of my frailty which makes me desire to be alone with Thee : and hence too my forgetfulness of Thy children.   Yet if in this I have offended Thee, humbly and in fear do I confess my fault."   " If thou hadst perfect charity," replied the Lord, "thou wouldst have entered in spirit into the sufferings I have borne for sinners and for My children whom I have redeemed." Margaret murmured ; " Lord, I know I have offended by want of charity ; yet it was from mere thoughtlessness, not from lack of desire.   For unceasingly in my heart do I desire and pray that Thou wouldst grant them full mercy."

Then said the Lord to her : " Have I not told thee thou art set in the world to be a light to the blind?   Whosoever has charity towards My children has charity towards Me. And now I would have thee tell My sons, the Friars, that when they preach they are not to talk about the birds of the air or otherwise vainly, but let them preach the words of the Gospels and Epistles. Nor should they care if people murmur against them, for so did they murmur against Me their Lord. Again, tell the Friars that I have given them larger nets and greater power in preaching the Gospel than I have given to other preachers. Wherefore I command them that they preach of My sufferings and death to the people, and when they preach let them suffer in their own souls as I suffered. For so will they turn sinners away from sin and draw them onwards to that blessed delight which I purchased for them at so great a cost. And let them warn sinners that of all vices, that is most offensive to Me which had its punishment in My own birth. For hell has sent forth new legions to worry the world, and preachers must needs be fervent and full of zeal." After this the Lord blessed Margaret in His accustomed manner, in the name of the Father, Son and Holy Ghost, and in the name of His most holy Mother.

LIII.

Margaret takes up her abode in the house under the Rocca. The parish priest's mistake is made known to her by Our Lord. He reassures her at her next Communion, and teaches her the value of detachment from earthly things. She is to meditate often upon the Manger and its poverty; upon our Lord's many labours and upon His betrayal and sufferings on the Cross. Why greater faith is experienced by Margaret in receiving Him at the hands of one priest rather than of another.—Leg. vii. 26, 27, 28.

It was on the first day of May that Margaret took up her abode in the house under the Rocca that she might the more easily avoid the company and gossip of the people who came to her. As soon as she arrived there she sent for Ser Giunta,* the aged parish priest of the Church of St. George, and having confessed to him, she besought him to bring her Communion the next morning. So at the appointed hour the priest came, bringing with him a pyx in which were unconsecrated hosts, and, as he thought, gave her Communion.

* This Ser Giunta must not be confused with Fra Giunta.

Now Margaret, feeling none of the sweetness of devotion to which she was accustomed when receiving the Sacred Host, thought it must be because of her own unworthiness, and was much distressed, and forthwith she besought our Lord to have pity upon her. But He, the Comforter of the sorrowing, spoke to her, saying : " My child, weep not ; for the priest did not give Me to thee, and so it was that thou didst not feel the joy of My presence."

Margaret, therefore, sent without delay for the priest and asked him why he had not brought her the Body of the Lord ; and he, in confusion, explained to her how, because of certain evil-doers who had robbed the Church of the Sacred Hosts, he now kept the Blessed Sacrament in his house, and how, near by, was a pyx containing unconsecrated hosts, which in his hurry and forgetfulness he had taken up by mistake.

After this Margaret was in great fear because of the priest's forgetfulness, and wished rather to go without Communion than that the same thing should happen again. Wherefore the next time she received Communion, the Eternal Lamb, wishing to put her mind at rest, revealed His presence to her, saying : " Behold, I am Jesus Christ, the

Son of the Living God, Who came into the world and took flesh of the Virgin Mary ; and dutifully do I salute her with an *Ave Maria.*" *

But the following day, when she again received the Holy Communion, she heard the Lord saying to her : " Thou dost wonder why it is I do not speak to thee as often as thou couldst wish. But ask thyself whether thy life is altogether pleasing to Me. I tell thee the desire with which thou dost desire Me is indeed acceptable to Me, yet dost thou displease Me somewhat because in thy anxiety about matters which are told thee or which thou hast thyself seen, thou art distracted when thou shouldst be thinking of Me alone."

Hearing this, Margaret exclaimed: "Thou knowest it is not for myself and the alms given me for my own maintenance that I am solicitous, for I desire but poverty ; but it is for my companion and the poor who come to me in their need, lest they suffer on my account and be scandalised."† The Lord answered : " Thou must never let thy thoughts become fixed on earthly and transi-

* " *Ave Maria usque Tui.*"
† "Ne de receptione rerum praebeatur deædificationis exemplum." This passage probably refers to the incident recorded on page 196.

tory affairs which, instead of raising thy mind to eternal things, cast it down into the dust; for thou canst not serve these things and Me."

Then Margaret: "My Lord, my Father, teach thine unworthy handmaiden what to love and what to think about, what to labour at and what to ponder upon, that I may be pleasing to Thy Majesty; for I know, and know well, that every good gift and every perfect gift proceeds from Thee, the Father of Lights, unto Thy children whom Thou didst create and whom with Thine own blood Thou hast redeemed; and Thou dost grant them Thy gifts in abundance, neither art Thou harsh with them."

After this the Lord said to her: "My child, meditate often upon the Manger, the cradle of Mine Infancy, and upon its poverty; meditate too upon My many labours, upon My last Supper and betrayal, and upon My sufferings on the Cross."

But still Margaret was much disturbed because, herself most reverent, she abhorred with all her soul the sin of irreverence. Therefore Christ spake again to her, saying: "My child, do not hesitate to receive Me from the hands of the priest, Ser Giunta, because when he brings thee Communion he seems lacking in reverence ; for the reverence of thine own heart is acceptable to Me.   His want of reverence displeases Me, yet the words of consecration ordained by Me, at the uttering of which I come down and dwell in this most august Sacrament—these words are not displeasing to Me.   If thou dost experience greater faith and devotion in receiving Me at the hands of one priest than at the hands of another, it is because I more freely impart My favours through those who are good than through those who are bad, and more clearly manifest My Presence."

LIV.

Margaret's desire for the greater enjoyment of the presence of Christ. Our Lord tells her this hunger is the mark of weak souls. She must think of those others for whose sake He has wrought such great things in her. Her acquiescence in all God may will for her. Our Lord teaches her to be detached and united to Him in the daily life of suffering which sinners inflict upon him. Margaret accuses herself of her faults. Our Lord tells her not to be anxious and solicitous, not to desire a perpetual Easter, but to prepare to endure a Lenten fast. Margaret prays for her Directors.—Leg. vii. 29.

Now one Saturday morning Margaret felt in herself a desire for a still greater enjoyment of the presence of Christ and besought the Lord to grant this her desire. But He said to her : "Thou dost ask great things, but art thou worthy of them?" Margaret exclaimed : "My Lord Christ, I am not worthy ; yet do I have recourse to Thy pity." Then said the Lord : "This hunger for the enjoyment of My Presence is but the sign of a weak soul. Thou must think of others, the children of My redemption ; for such graces as I have given thee are not for thy sake alone, but for the sake of them who still crucify Me. And yet in My fatherly love for them I humble Myself that I may bring them back to Me.   But thou hast no care but to satisfy thine own hunger, and art forgetful of the children for whose sake I have wrought great things in thee.*"

Margaret humbly replied : "My Lord, if it is for the greater good of Thy children, lead me back into the early days of Thy gracious intercourse when thou didst speak to them through me.   But I fear, my Lord, Thou hast become my confessor : wherefore, O Eternal Priest, do I accuse myself to Thee of all my negligences."   And forthwith she began to accuse herself of her faults.   But Christ said: "Nay, not to Me alone shalt thou confess thy faults, but to thy confessor also. I would have thee remember the lepers and how I sent them to the priests to be cleansed."†

Now as Margaret was thus making confession to Christ the Lord, she was filled with great gladness because of His presence, and she exclaimed : "My Lord, how could Thy Mother bear the joy of Thy Presence when she became Thy Mother at the Angel's word ? "   And the Lord : "As in My power and wisdom I willed her to be My Mother,

---

* Compare this chapter with St. Margaret's prayers that Our Lord would not grant her favours in the presence of others, chap. xxiv.

† Luke xvii. 14.

so did I enable her to bear it." Again, after this, the Lord said to her : "What wouldst thou : that I be to thee a Father, and thou, nevertheless, be not a child to Me ; or that thou shouldst be to Me a child and I not a Father to thee ? " At first Margaret was puzzled to know how to reply, but being inwardly enlightened by the Divine Master himself, she answered : "My Lord, I choose to be to Thee a child, for Thou art in very deed a Father to all Thy creatures." Then the Lord : "Keep careful guard over thy soul, for thou art the instrument of My mercy." And Margaret : "Careful indeed must be the guard I keep, O Lord !" The Lord : " To keep careful guard over thyself thou must needs separate thyself from the world." Margaret cried out : " But Lord, even when I separate myself from the world I serve Thee badly." To this the Lord made answer : " It is better to struggle against the temptations from within thee than to flee from them and keep company with the world ; for in thy struggles with thyself thy soul is purified ; but if thou dost linger in the world, thy mind becomes busy with vain imaginings, and when I come to seek rest in thy soul I find it already occupied and its purity dimmed, and so thou dost cease to live with Me the daily life of suffering which sinners inflict upon Me."

In this moment of sweet accusation, Margaret was shown clearly all her faults and the places where she had offended.

And because she no longer enjoyed the consolations of her earlier days, she asked: "Lord, why is it I am no longer sensible of the joys of Thy Kingdom?" And this was the Lord's reply: "I deal with thee as I find thee. At present thy mind is almost wholly taken up with the affairs of those who come to thee." Then Margaret: "Lord, let me retire into solitude." Christ answered: "Now I am indeed to thee a Father, but thou art not to Me a child." Margaret exclaimed: "Truly, Lord, do I know that it is for the sake of Thy children Thou hast bestowed on me such immense favours, Thou Who art the Joy of Angels and the Delight of the Blessed."

As she uttered these words her soul was filled with such sweetness that, as she herself explained, if she had been cast into flames for punishment, yet would she not grieve that the Lord rebuked her. Again, therefore, Margaret said: "Lord, so great is the joy I find in Thy Presence that beside it all things in heaven and earth pass into nothing; for as soon as Thou art near all trouble vanishes, and I learn things no words can utter. Wherefore, O Fire which never smoulderest, I desire to be enkindled by Thee, and I would that I knew how great is Thy love for me."

Once more the Lord rebuked her : " Margaret," He said, "canst thou think of nothing but thyself? " Margaret made answer : " My Lord, since Thou hast said this hunger of my soul is a sign of weakness, I beseech Thee make me strong."

Then spoke the Lord: " I have already given thee a strengthening medicine which thou hast but little used; namely, that thou shouldst cast out thy fears and restrain thy desires, and for love of Me be not solicitous about thy body. Thou desirest a perpetual Easter, but thou must needs endure a Lenten fast. And I would have thee bear in mind the example of that servant whose lord remitted to him five hundred pence; who afterwards himself refused to remit to his fellow-servant a debt of fifty pence. So do thou not forget My children."

After that Margaret besought the Lord on behalf of the two Fathers, her directors, and she received this reply : " Say to them from Me : ' Blessed are the clean of heart, for they shall see Me face to face.' "

LV.

Margaret learns by revelation of a poor family much in need of clothing. Christ commands her to send her new gown to them. She does so with great joy.—Leg. viii. 1.

Now to Margaret, as we have said, the poor were as her own children, and she watched over them with a mother's love and was full of zeal for their salvation. One day (it was winter, and because of the cold Margaret had put on a new coarse gown, and, feeling very weak, was lying on her bed of twigs) the Lord revealed to her that in a certain village, some miles distant from the city, there was a poor man who had a large family of children too young to work or make themselves useful; and they were much in need of food and clothing, but the man was ashamed to beg. Wherefore Christ, the Beloved, commanded her without delay to find means to send her new gown to this poor family. "Lord," exclaimed Margaret, "willingly would I give my very soul to the poor if I might!" And with great joy she at once took off her gown and sent it to the poor family.

LVI.

Fra Giunta asks for Margaret's prayers, the French forces being assembled outside Forli. In answer to her prayer, it is revealed to her that the armies would not fight. Shortly afterwards Pope Nicholas III. intervened.—Leg. viii. 2.

Another time when the French forces* assembled to fight against the people of Forli, and much bloodshed was expected, the writer of these acts went to this indefatigable advocate for sinners, and besought her to pray for the combatants on both sides. And when she had prayed, behold those words of the Psalm were fulfilled: "The Just shall cry out and the Lord will hear them." For immediately it was revealed to her that, owing to the intervention of a neighbouring power, the armies would not fight. And so it came to pass, for shortly afterwards Pope Nicholas III., of pious memory, inhibited the war, and, as had been revealed to her, the movements of the armies ceased.

* In the threatened war between Charles of Anjou and the Emperor in 1279.—Muratori, *Annali d' Italia*, vol. xi.

LVII.

*The souls of the dead permitted to come to ask
Margaret's aid. Two brothers from Cortona come.
Our Lord instructs Margaret to tell the Friars to
remember the souls of the dead. Those of them
who mix themselves in worldly affairs will have
much to suffer in purgatory.*—Leg. viii. 5.

But Christ, leading Margaret in the broad
ways of charity, not only sent to her numbers
of people from far-off lands, but permitted
even the souls of the dead to come and ask
her aid in their suffering. Thus, to take one
instance among several, there were two
brothers from Cortona who had been killed,
and they appeared to Margaret and said to
her: "Although we were unable to confess
our sins before dying, yet as we were being
led through the wood by the robbers we
foresaw that they were taking us to death,
and, by the mercy of our Maker, we were
suddenly taken with sorrow for our sins, and
in this sorrow we bore patiently the cruel
death the robbers inflicted on us, and so we
escaped the eternal fires. But we were both

day - labourers, and both — but especially I who am speaking to you—dishonest in our labour.   Wherefore, I beseech you, most pitiful mother, take what things you find in my house and, as far as you can, make satisfaction to those for whom I worked, especially the people on the hill-side ; and do the same for this my brother who is with me."

Now whilst Margaret was praying for these two and others, the Lord said to her : " Tell the Friars Minor that they ever bear in mind the souls of the dead who suffer for their sins in purgatory, for they are a vast multitude beyond the thought of man, and they are helped but little by those on earth, even by those who are dear to them ; and tell the Friars also that those of them who occupy themselves with worldly affairs will have much to suffer in purgatory."

LVIII.

Margaret prays for a Friar who is in great bitterness of soul. Our Lord gives her a message for her confessor about him. Margaret is told to go on working for sinners. Our Lord further promises that He will put the saving word of grace into her mouth.—Leg. viii. 6, 7.

Again, on the feast of the Virgin St. Clare, Margaret was praying for a Friar who was in great bitterness of soul and almost desperate, when the Father of all clemency spoke to her and bade her tell her confessor to go in His Name and induce the Superior to take pity upon the poor friar, who was as a stone in the mortar, ready to be hurled forth. And he added: "If the Superior is grieved because of the offence against Me which this Friar has committed, let him bear in mind the words I spoke to St. Peter: 'I say not to thee seven times but even unto seventy times seven times!' * Wherefore it is My will that he have mercy upon this weakling, and that he himself afterwards make reparation to Me for all who offend Me."

* Matthew xviii., 22.

And on the feast of the SS. Chrysanthus and Daria, Christ spoke to Margaret after she had received Holy Communion, saying : " My child, however hard be thine own sufferings, cease not from endeavouring to root out vice from the heart of the sinner and to plant therein the seed of virtue.   Scatter the good seed, and I will give thee seed to scatter, for I will put the saving word of grace into thy mouth.   And even though I should cease to converse with thee, yet will I continue to enlighten thee that thy words may be true."

LIX.

Our Saviour gives Margaret a most comforting message for her confessor, Fra Giunta.—Leg. viii. 8.

Now, at the time that Fra Giunta, her confessor, was dwelling in Siena, the Saviour appeared to Margaret one day when she was in prayer and commanded her : " Write to thy confessor thus : God the Father to His son, blessing and the intimate approval which is for His children whom He has redeemed at great price, especially those who have once wandered from His path. Increase in all grace that whatsoever in thee is of God may always tend to God, and that the light which is given thee may be used for the purpose of thy Creator. For I, the Most High and only God, will to honour my friends both on earth and in heaven. Wherefore let it not seem hard to thee, My son, to have to labour for Me ; but remember how I, too, was often weary, and that I have prepared for thee a great reward, and then thy labours will be pleasant and thy weariness will be to thee an unspeakable gladness. The wine-cup which thy friend Franco saw in spirit when he prayed for thee signifies the sacrifice of thy God's own labours,* because thou dost carry My Name with ardent devotion to a stiff-necked people. The cross put into thy hands invites thee often to come unto My cross. And the rose which was given thee signifies most spotless chastity, the perfume of which covers even one's friends. Wherefore, as a father teaching his son, I teach thee that when thou preachest to the people thou shouldst be gentle and sympathetic with sinners, and in warning them against sin thou must not fail at the same time to tell them of the loving Mercy which I extend to the sinner who comes back to Me. For thyself, My son, do thou maintain gravity of manners amidst all thy works, for I shall be always with thee unless thou losest Me by thine own fault. And now I bless Thee in the Name of the Father, of Myself and of the Holy Ghost, and in the name of the most blessed Virgin Mary, from whom I deigned to take flesh that all men might be saved."

* This evidently refers to some vision in which Franco saw a wine-cup offered to Fra Giunta, together with a cross and a rose. Some critics have read Franciscus for Francus in the text and supposed the name referred to the Seraphic Saint; but Da Pelago and Crivelli maintain that Francus or Franco referred to a person living at Cortona. Fra Giunta was sent away from Cortona to Siena in 1290.

LX.

*Margaret prays for the citizens of Cortona.
Our Lord's instructions to her confessor for their
good. The enemy of souls appears to Margaret and
tells her he will fight against her confessor. He
does so, and but for the timely aid of Christ the
confessor would have feared to continue his work.
The enemy sows discord between Margaret and her
confessor. Margaret, continuing to pray for him,
receives a consoling message from Our Lord for
him, and is told what he is to say to the people of
Cortona. Our Lord tells her that her confessor will
suffer in this world through his efforts for peace,
but shall thereby find mercy in his last hour.—
Leg. viii. 12, 13, 14.*

Now, Margaret was one day beseeching the
Giver of Peace on behalf of the turbulent
citizens of Cortona when she obtained this
reply: "My child, tell thy confessor that he
should first strive to establish concord between the inhabitants of the city themselves;
and afterwards let him labour for peace between Cortona and the neighbouring cities.
And tell him that the time will come when
the citizens will remember his words and
receive them more readily than now."

At this time it happened that the confessor
was labouring to put an end to a private feud,
and the devil appeared to Margaret and said

to her : " Know that I will fight against thy confessor in his endeavour to establish peace in the city." And behold how it came to pass ; for he dealt the confessor such a hurt that but for the timely aid of Christ, the protector of those who trust in Him, the confessor would have feared to continue his work. But the Good Physician, listening to the prayers which Margaret poured forth on her confessor's behalf, sent him His blessing as a father to a son; telling the confessor not to fear, for that He, the Lord Christ, was with him. And thus was the confessor strengthened to continue his labours for peace.

But the enemy of souls sought yet to sow discord, for now he excited the confessor against Margaret because, as it seemed to him, she was indiscreet in her austerities ; and for many days he even ceased to visit her. Still Margaret, with great sweetness of soul, continued to pray for him, and one day after communion she heard Christ say to her: " Tell thy confessor I wish his life to be that of an apostle, and let him find comfort in Me and bring to Me all his troubles. And when he sets himself to guide souls, let him not be too anxious, nor shall he take heed when people murmur against him, for so did many murmur bitterly against Me, their Creator. And let him diligently consider how many came to crucify Me in the hour of My passion who afterwards came to adore Me. Wherefore let him not draw back from his labours but continue therein to the end, seeking to establish peace in the city : for I am with him."

Another day Christ said to Margaret : "My child, what wouldst thou say if the time came that the citizens of Cortona should bless the alms they give thee, seeing that thou art set as a voice in the wilderness to call them to peace ? For I will that thou cry 'Peace amongst men' unto Cortona ; and truly art thou sent as a messenger of peace. And this grace do I grant to the citizens of Cortona because of the reverent devotion they have shown thee. Wherefore tell thy confessor to preach publicly in Cortona the message of peace and in My Name to invite the people to mutual trust and concord."*

But Margaret feared to be deluded by the dark enemy who sometimes takes on an appearance of virtue ; therefore she replied : "My Lord Jesus Christ, Thou true Peace ! do Thou Thyself make peace and choose

---

* The "message of peace" was the burden of Franciscan preaching throughout the xiiith century. See *The Friars, and How They came to England*, intro. 95.

another to be Thy messenger, and not me."
The Lord answered her : " My child, thou
voice in the wilderness, do as I bid thee and
see thou tell thy confessor that he with confidence invite the people to make peace ; and
let him recall to their mind how I, the Creator
of all things that are, the Lord Almighty,
made peace with My persecutors. He shall
tell them how I made peace with those who
delivered Me up to Mine enemies and with
those who derided Me and tore off My
garments and scourged Me ; how I made
peace with those who spat in My face and
struck Me ; with those who blindfolded Me
and crowned Me with thorns ; who crucified
Me and gave Me vinegar to drink and who
pierced My side ; aye, even with those who
denied me. Let them consider how I thus
made peace when, because of the bitterness
of My sufferings, My human nature, so
sensitively formed, was nigh to break. Therefore do I command the people of Cortona to
put aside all feuds whatsoever and make
peace forthwith, lest, contemning My words
of mercy, they fall under the judgment of My
wrath."

Then Margaret exclaimed : " But, Lord,
does not my unworthiness come between my
prayer and Thee, as a cloud between the

earth and the sun ? " The Lord answered : " I tell thee, announce the words of peace, calling upon Cortona to lay aside its quarrels, for their defects will in nowise hinder their peace. For I, thy Redeemer, have put thee in the wilderness of this world as a voice crying aloud. Thine early life did indeed cry out against me ; but now brought into the way of penance, thy life cries aloud that I am full of mercy ; and sinners hear and learn from thee."

Again, some time afterwards the Lord spake to Margaret and said to her : " My child, thou knowest that thy confessor on Friday last made peace between some of the citizens, and this was pleasing to Me ; but it would have been more pleasing had he obeyed My command at once to set himself to bring about the peace. I, the Son of God, in the hour of My passion did not delay but rose up at once, saying to My Apostles : ' Let us arise and go hence.' It is true that if this Christ-bearer, thy confessor, had not delayed, he would that day have tasted of My passion. Even so, however, he will not escape suffering, for because of the peace he has brought about there is suffering to come to him ; but he will thereby find mercy in his last hour."

LXI.

A confessor in doubt as to questioning his penitents asks Margaret's prayers for light. Our Lord's reply. The blindness sin brings into the soul. Another Friar, in doubt as to how often he should say Mass, asks for prayers. Our Lord commends him for his compassion and zeal for the poor.—Leg. viii. 16 ; ix. 6.

There was a confessor, Fra Filippo by name, who was in doubt whether he ought to question the penitents who came to confess to him, for he was afraid lest they should foolishly misunderstand his questioning. Wherefore because of shame he had failed to question those who hid their sins from him. At length he came to Margaret's confessor, and besought him to ask her to pray that the Lord would show him how to act in this matter. And the Lord, hearing her prayer, said : " Tell Fra Filippo in My name that he may without danger hear confessions and question his penitents. For there are diversities of graces amongst men ; and this grace of hearing confessions

and questioning penitents is granted to him
because of his purity of mind and body.
Therefore, if a thousand people should come
to confession to him in one day he must not
refuse to hear one of them, nor fail to
question any one whom he has reason to
think needs to be questioned. Oftentimes
sinners do not confess their sins because, in
the blindness of mind which sin brings upon
them, they do not see their sin.   And this is
their own fault, since by the evil odour of
their lives they have driven Me away Who
am the true Light.   And so it becomes
necessary, My child, that confessors should
question sinners concerning their sins.   For
this I love the Friars Minor, because they
have a zeal and holy solicitude for souls, and
by their labours bring back many souls to
life."

Another Friar, Benigno in deed and name,
was in doubt as to how often he should say
Mass, and merited to obtain through Margaret this reply from the Lord : " Tell Fra
Benigno, who fears to receive the Sacrament
of My Body and Blood too frequently, that
I permit him to celebrate frequently ; only
before he goes to the altar let him make a
full confession of all his sins and cast out all
perturbation of soul.   And I command him

to persevere to the end in that compassion for the poor which he now has ; for much does it please Me that he goes seeking out the poor, the sick, and the ailing in their own homes, and that he is more anxious to bring these to confession than he is to bring the rich ones of the world." For Fra Benigno was so solicitous for the poor in their necessities that he not only procured for them all he could but even denied himself the necessary things of life that he might, with leave of his Superior, supply their wants.

LXII

After Communion, Our Lord tells Margaret to admonish the Bishop of Arezzo in what and how he is to amend, and commands him to study without delay the rule of life which every bishop should observe. Six days later, after Communion, Our Lord tells Margaret to again speak to the Bishop. Margaret's letter of advice to her son. His fault. His petulant repentance. Margaret knows from God what had happened and sends begging she may see her son. He comes to her cell with Fra Ubertino. She instructs and corrects him and then sends him back to the convent.—Leg. viii. 17; ix. 27.

Now this daughter of the Most High, knowing how the ancient enemy never rests in seeking out souls to their deadly injury, wrote this letter to her son, from whom she had parted for the love of Christ :

" My son, blessed be thou of the Lord, to Whose service thou hast bound thyself ; and if for His sake thou fightest valiantly, thou wilt ever find me loving towards thee, and I will be thy mother indeed if thou observest what I now teach thee. And in the first place I exhort thee by the love of Christ to plant in thy soul the obedience of most profound humility, and to do in all gentleness the behests of all the brethren of the Order, giving to each the reverence due to his grade without distinction of persons. Next I would have thee be modest as one grateful to God concerning thine own gifts, reverent and upright, never presuming to murmur against others. And according to the custom of thy most holy Order, be plain and simple ; fly from useless intercourse with worldlings, but keep company with thy brethren and with holy men. Let thy prayers, my son, be always fervent, and do thou have a vigilant care to stand always prepared against the multiform snares of thine enemy. Never conceal from thy confessor anything which ought to be manifested to him : for the sick man cannot be cured unless he shows the physician his wounds. Faithfully, and in all meekness, receive the advice of those wiser than thyself, and prefer their counsel to that of thine own heart, as being more profitable to thee. Recite the hours of the Divine Office reverently in the presence of the Lord without distraction of mind or restlessness of body ; and do not put off thine office beyond the time determined by the Church and do not omit any part of it. When any one of

the brethren corrects thee for thy faults,
immediately bare thy head and fall upon thy
knees, and, shutting thy heart against any intrusion of obstinacy, humbly confess thy fault.
If thou art ever in trouble take courage from
the remembrance of thy crucified Lord ; and
willingly accept the commands of thy superior
as the commands of the Lord Himself.
Against the sin of evil words, set upon thy
lips two towers of defence, namely, purity
and courtesy.   Be slow to speak, but when
thou speakest let thy words be few and
weighty.   Watch over thy thoughts in their
very inception ; and in all thy acts beware
lest thou do injury to God.   And that thou
mayest keep thyself pure in the service of
God, have a guard upon thy senses.

"Keep this letter which I send thee until
thy death, and often read it and endeavour
always to carry out the lessons it contains."

But one night the son of Margaret was
overcome with sleep, so that when the Friars
rose at the midnight hour to recite Matins he
did not rise with them.   And the guardian
went to arouse him, and, like a father with
his son, gave him a blow with a stick.
Whereupon the youth, springing up, cried
out ; and he seized the stick and wrenched it
from the hands of the guardian.   But im-

mediately he repented him of his fault and began to beat himself with the hood of his tunic.

Now when it was dawn Margaret arose, and knowing from God what had happened, sent a messenger to the guardian before the signal for Prime, beseeching him to allow her to see her son without delay. He came, therefore, accompanied by Fra Ubertino, to his mother's cell, and she said to him with tears in her eyes: "My son, my soul was present with thee this night when thou didst cry out and seize the stick from thy guardian and beat thyself in childish fashion with thy hood. My son, whither has thy fervour flown, for thou wert fervent in the Divine praises? And where is thy gratitude for so good a father?" And having thus spoken to him for his correction and instruction, she sent him back to the convent.

LXIII.

Our Lord after Communion compassionates Margaret in her sufferings and tells her it is for love of her He shows mercy to the double-dealing, deceitful people of Cortona. Margaret's self-abasement. A lay-brother, who finds everything but prayer burdensome to him and injurious to his soul, begs Margaret's prayers. He desires to receive Holy Communion every eight days, but fears to presume, and asks Margaret's advice. Our Lord says he is to receive every fifteen days, not because of his defects but that he may the more long for Him. He tells him to keep His cross before his soul and thereon let himself be crucified. He promises him daily Communion later on.—Leg. ix. 28.

There was a certain lay-brother, beloved of God and his brethren, who was so given to the exercise of prayer that everything seemed burdensome to him and injurious to his soul except to pray, to recite the Divine praises and to listen to sermons. Amongst other things he greatly desired to receive the Holy Communion once every week, but because of the sublimity of the Divine Majesty and his own lowliness he would not presume to receive so frequently until he had sought the advice of Margaret. She therefore prayed for him ; and when she had prayed she heard Christ say to her : " My child, tell the brother that he is to receive Me, his Creator, once every fifteen days : such is My pleasure. Nor do I make this rule because of any notable defects in him, but that he may thirst the more for Me and receive Me the more hungrily. And when at any time he desires to receive Me and may not, let him remember the words of the holy doctor of the Church who said: 'Believe and thou hast eaten.' Wherefore let him prepare his soul for new graces and strive to amend his faults and to cast out all sin. And wheresoever he may be, whether in the dormitory or the cloister, in the kitchen or the refectory, or in any other place, let him always keep before his soul My cross ; and thereon let him be crucified with Me; and from this fount there shall flow forth for him not only the graces he prays for but others he might well pray for. And let him take comfort, for the time will come when he shall communicate every day ; and at that time he will no longer serve in the kitchen." And so it came to pass.

LXIV.

Christ entrusts Margaret with messages for the Bishop of Arezzo.—Leg. ix. 43, 44.

It was the fifth day of May* that Christ said to Margaret after Communion : " My child, I command thee to send word to the Bishop of Arezzo that he must give up all those revenues of the Church which belong to the poor, and that he must not league himself with the factions which divide the people of Tuscany. Tell him he must no longer continue to spend money at the Roman Court, sojourning there without need and beyond the canonical times ; nor should he any longer take counsel with his relatives. But let him come in all humility to thee, and I will put right and timely counsel into thy mouth concerning him. Tell him to disgorge the ill-gotten gains which are made at his court, which by right should be My court, where all should be taken and given according to law. And he must cease from taking part in the wars waged by his family in their

* A.D. 1277.—Concerning this Bishop of Arezzo, Guglielmo Ubertini, see Ughelli, *Italia Sacra*, vol. i., p. 423.

own interest. Tell him that though he believes he is increasing the rights and dignity of his episcopate, yet he can neither increase nor even maintain them if he walks not according to My Will. If he is involved in war it is because for a long time he has lived to My displeasure. Let him, then, without delay study the rule of life which every bishop should observe, for certainly hitherto he has observed no episcopal rule whatever nor lived according to canonical law. Tell him he is to blame for that in the wars mothers were burnt with their children, whom I redeemed at a great price in My passion. And I will not permit his favourite palace to be desolated by fire lest the fire, having taken its revenge, shall have no second judgment in store for him afterwards. Wherefore I bid him without delay make peace with all men."

After six days the Lord again spoke to Margaret after she had received Holy Communion : " My child, tell the Bishop of Arezzo again that his castles, which should be centres of peace and divine praise, must no longer be held to spread war and carry death to Christian peoples ; for many are the souls that have been sent to perdition by these wars."

LXV.

Christ has the same compassion for Margaret as He had for Mary and Martha. In Margaret His life is revealed afresh. He would punish the Cortonese for their sins, but shows mercy for love of Margaret. Margaret's small opinion of herself: she fears even her Lord, and has no confidence in her merits.—Leg. x. 12.

But one day during the octave of the Ascension, Margaret heard Christ saying to her after Communion : " My child, my chosen one, I grieve with thee in thy sufferings, though in Myself I can neither grieve nor suffer; but ever in the presence of My Eternal Father I plead for thee with that compassion which I had for Mary and Martha in their trouble; for in thee My life is revealed afresh. And I tell thee that daily do the people of Cortona offend Me by their double-dealings and deceit, even as does the entire world ; and did I regard only them, their sins would excite My wrath to punish them ; but for love of thee I show them mercy."

And yet Margaret esteemed herself as utterly wanting and without virtue. Wherefore the Lord rebuked her, saying : " O incredulous one ! " She replied : " Lord, truly do I confess Thee to be Infinite patience ; and whatsoever Thou dost will Thou canst do. It is not because of Thee, therefore, that I doubt, but because of mine own unworthiness ; for my faults make me in every way diffident of myself and cause me to fear even Thee and to lose all confidence in mine own merits."

LXVI.

Margaret, weeping over her inability to serve the Lord as she had promised, is greatly comforted by one of her companions speaking sweetly about God. She begs Our Lord to come to her in spirit. He hears her prayer and blesses her, promising that at her death many will strike their breasts in sorrow for their sins.—Leg. xi. 12.

One Sunday during paschal-tide Margaret was weeping because it seemed to her she could not serve the Lord as she had promised, when one of her companions began to speak sweetly about God, and this greatly comforted her. Whereupon, with her heart on fire, she besought the Lord to come to her in spirit. And He Who said : "Seek and ye shall find," heard His handmaid's prayer. And He said to her : "What wouldst thou, My child ? Fear not, for I, thy Creator, am with thee." But Margaret was afraid, for she thought her life must be displeasing to God since, on account of her bodily weakness, she was unable to perform her accustomed services. Wherefore, to quieten her fears, Christ invited her to ask for a blessing in the Name of the Eternal Father. And when she had asked this blessing Christ said to her : "And I, thy Lord, bless thee in all thy works." But the humble Margaret, reputing her good works to be nothing, asked : "What are my works, O Lord ? " The Lord answered her : " My child, thine eating and drinking, thy waking and sleeping, thy silence and thy speaking, and all thy life is a prayer in My sight because of thy desire to serve Me and thy fear of offending Me. And therefore I bless thee, and not only thee but the cell in which thou livest, for thou art a new light in the world. And I say to thee that thou art as the rose amongst flowers ; thou art pure, and because of the purity which thou lovest thou art placed amongst the virgins ; and at thy death many will strike their breast in sorrow for their sins."

XLVII.

An angel appearing to Margaret blesses her and her cell. Margaret calls her companions to praise the Lord. Our Lord tells Margaret how to plead for sinners. Margaret asks what she shall do in order to live in her Lord to the end. Our Lord tells her to keep a pure mind and subject herself not only to Him but also to all creatures. He tells her she is the third light granted to the Order of His beloved Francis. Margaret's Angel tells her the Seraph has left her two gifts: the fire of love and the knowledge of God.—Leg. ix. 35 ; xi. 9.

One night—it was the second Sunday of Advent and the hour of matins—the hand-maiden of Christ was praising God, when she beheld above her cell an Angel of fiery countenance, having six wings, who sweetly and readily blessed her and her cell. Where-upon she herself was touched by the fire of the flaming Angel, and with much fervour called upon her companions who were with her, as well as upon her household and neigh-bours, to come and praise the Lord Who had sent so noble an Angel. And together they praised in the Angel the Creator of Angels. Then Margaret, transfigured and absorbed in the love of the loving God, became as one dead, so that her companions had to uphold her.

Then said the Lord to Margaret : " Thou art she who wages a great war against Mine enemy. And I say to thee, my people, turning their thoughts from Me, have forgotten Me, neither do they care aught for Me. Yet, though they hold Me so cheaply and offend me greatly, I do not accuse them before My Father as I do before thee, nor do I recite their offences to Him that so He may punish and destroy them, but I am their advocate Who seek to reverse their sentence. And yet I tell thee, sinners suffer bitter pains ; and wars and dangers, famine and pestilence will come upon them before their time is finished."

Then Margaret asked : " My Lord, what shall I do that I may live to the end in Thee? For because of the great sweetness I have tasted I am become bold, and do not consider Thy greatness with due fear, nor do I think of mine own lowliness." The Lord replied : " My child, keep a pure mind. And because that thy prayer was pleasing to Me when thou didst pray thou mightest be subject to all creatures, I command thee henceforth to subject thyself not only to Me but to all creatures in so far as it will redound to My glory, and for love of Me to hold thyself contemptible in the sight of all mankind, imitating my example ; for I made Myself subject to all men and willed that they should hold me in contempt.   And this humble lowering of thyself will exalt thee amongst the blessed who are in heaven.   And be thou white in thine innocence and ruddy in thy love ; for thou art the third light granted to the Order of My beloved Francis.   He is the first light, shining in the Order of the Friars Minor ; the Blessed Clare is the second light, shining in the order of the Nuns ; and thou art the third light, in the order of the Penitents."

But when this glorious colloquy was over, a little while afterwards Margaret's guardian Angel stood by her and said : " The Angel of the Seraphic choir who came down to thee has left thee the fire of love and the splendour of the high knowledge of God."

LXVIII.

Why many things remain unwritten concerning the handmaid of the Lord. The day, hour and manner of her passing hence are revealed to Margaret. An eminent soul, rapt in prayer, beholds the spirit of Margaret taken up to Heaven with a multitude of souls newly released from purgatory. Margaret's body is buried in a new sepulchre. Here, according to the promises made to Margaret by God, many miracles are wrought.—Leg. xi. 20.

Now, many things there are which are not written concerning the handmaid of the Lord, both because of her own humility which caused her to hide the secret of God and also because that for seven years her confessor, who wrote these things, was absent from Cortona.

But as her life drew near its end, Margaret prayed ever more earnestly to be released from the bondage of this world; and the most merciful Saviour, listening to her prayers, hastened to grant her desire. And not only did He reveal to her long before the time the year and month and day of her passing hence, but He even foretold to her the happy and gladsome hour, to wit, the hour nearest the dawn, when she would go forth joyously to Christ in company with a multitude of happy souls and without having to pass through the purgatorial fires. Whereupon she began to lose the use of her bodily powers, and for seventeen days was unable to take bodily food, so that her strength faded away.   But on the feast of the See of St. Peter the Apostle, on the 8th of the Kalends of March, in the year of our Lord 1297, she passed unto the heavens, her face being as the face of an Angel, full of triumphant gladness.

Then all who stood by were sensible of a sweet and wondrous perfume, and they knew of a truth that Margaret had been a vessel of holiness containing all manner of heavenly graces.   And in that same hour a certain eminent soul was rapt in contemplation in Città di Castello, and his spirit beheld the spirit of Margaret, beaming with ineffable joy, taken up into heaven, together with a multitude of souls newly released from purgatory.   And from that day this person spoke of Margaret as Christ's second Magdalene.

Now, when the people of Cortona heard of the death of Margaret, calling together a council of the citizens, they went to the church of St. Basil and there, her body having been embalmed and clothed in a purple robe, they buried it in a new sepulchre, many clerics and religious being present. And here, according to the promises made her by God, many miracles were wrought.

THE END.

Made in the USA
San Bernardino, CA
22 February 2017